D0933393

COOL GUIDE
Paris

teNeues

Imprint

Editor: Nathalie Grolimund

Photos (location): © Barlotti (Barlotti), © Colette (Colette), © John Galliano (John Galliano), © Louis Vuitton (Louis Vuitton), © Printemps (Printemps), Benoit Autissier (The Ice Kube by Grey Goose), Roland Bauer (Baccarat, p.19, Bar du Murano Resort Paris, Bar du Plaza, Café de Flore, Café de l'Homme, Le Train Bleu, Market), Yann Deret (La Cantine du Faubourg), Pep Escoda (Café Marly, Costes, Georges, Kong, Maison Blanche), Joachim Frydman (Barrio Latino, Black Calvados, Champ de Mars, Culture Bière, Espace Kiliwatch, Ginger, Ladurée, Le Saut du Loup, Regine's, Restaurant BON, Le Sens, Showcase, Wochdom), Matthias Just (Centre Georges Pompidou, Cimetière du Père Lachaise, Côté Bastide, Galeries Lafayette, Jardin du Luxembourg, La Villette, Cité des Sciences, Marches du Sacré-Cœur, Musée Rodin, Palais de Tokyo, Place des Vosges, Puces de St-Ouen-Clignancourt, Salons du Palais Royal Shiseido, Viaduc des Arts), Claude Weber (Baccarat p.17/18), Anne Wencelius (Maison Blanche)

Cover Photo (location): Joachim Frydman (Barrio Latino)

Back cover photos from top to bottom (location): Pep Escoda (Kong), Joachim Frydman (Ladurée), © Printemps (Printemps), Joachim Frydman (Espace Kiliwatch)

Price categories: € = reasonable, €€ = moderate, €€€ = upscale, €€€€ = expensive

Introduction, texts: Elke Buscher. Layout & Pre-press, Imaging: fusion publishing. Translations: Übersetzungsbüro RR Communications: English: Robert Rosenbaum, Christie Tam; French: Lisa Caprano, Stéphane Gödde; Spanish: Bruno Plaza, Romina Russo

Produced by fusion publishing GmbH, Berlin   www.fusion-publishing.com

Published by teNeues Publishing Group

teNeues Verlag Gmbh + Co. KG
Am Selder 37
47906 Kempen, Germany
Tel.: 0049-(0)2152-916-0
Fax: 0049-(0)2152-916-111
E-mail: books@teneues.de

Press department:
arehn@teneues.de
Tel.: 0049-2152-916-202

teNeues Publishing Company
16 West 22nd Street
New York, NY 10010, USA
Tel.: 001-212-627-9090
Fax: 001-212-627-9511

teNeues Publishing UK Ltd.
York Villa, York Road
Byfleet
KT14 7HX, Great Britain
Tel.: 0044-1932-403509
Fax: 0044-1932-403514

teNeues France S.A.R.L.
93, rue Bannier
45000 Orléans, France
Tel.: 0033-2-38541071
Fax: 0033-2-38625340

www.teneues.com

ISBN: 978-3-8327-9295-4

© 2009 teNeues Verlag GmbH + Co. KG, Kempen

Printed in Italy

Bibliographic information published by the Deutsche Nationalbibliothek.

The Deutsche Nationalbibliothek lists this publication in the Deutsche Nationalbibliografie; detailed bibliographic data are available in the Internet at http://dnb.d-nb.de.

RESTAURANTS & CAFÉS

CLUBS, LOUNGES & BARS

SHOPS

HIGHLIGHTS

SERVICE

Introduction

"World-class city on the Seine"—Paris more than lives up to the reputation. Paris has, after all, been considered the art capital of Europe for more than 100 years. Museum after museum testify to this, either in historic palaces or in modern buildings specifically designed for art.

There are now some museums where in addition to French art and culture you can learn about French cuisine, which has likewise contributed to Paris's international reputation like at "Café de l'Homme" in the Palais de Chaillot or "Café Marly" in the world's largest museum, the Louvre. Award-winning chefs assemble in droves in Paris, and they long ago ceased being content with French cuisine alone, refining it nowadays with all manner of international influences. These pleasures are often served on upper floors, such as at the futuristic "Georges" on the upper level of Centre Pompidou, or at "Maison Blanche" near the Champs-Elysées—with a view of the city and its world-famous symbol, the Eiffel Tower.

You might go shopping beforehand in the big department stores from the 19th century, "Printemps" or "Galeries Lafayette," and admire the marvelous art nouveau glass cupolas. A wholly different strain of Parisian chic is found in vintage stores like "Espace Kiliwatch" and "Wochdom," where extensive rummaging is welcomed.

One thing you definitely should not miss is sitting in the Jardin du Luxembourg or on Place des Vosges in the happening Marais district to enjoy Parisian *savoir vivre*.

Elke Buscher

Einleitung

„Weltstadt an der Seine" – diesem Ruf wird Paris mehr als gerecht. Denn seit über 100 Jahren gilt Paris als die Kunstmetropole Europas. Zahlreiche Museen zeugen davon, entweder in historischen Palästen oder in modernen Gebäuden, die extra für die Kunst konzipiert wurden.

Inzwischen kann man in einigen Museen neben der französischen Kunst und Kultur auch die französische Küche kennen lernen, die ebenfalls zum Pariser Weltruf beigetragen hat – so wie im „Café de l'Homme" im Palais de Chaillot oder dem „Café Marly" im Louvre, dem größten Museum der Welt. Sterneköche tummeln sich zuhauf in Paris, und sie begnügen sich längst nicht mehr nur mit der französischen Küche, sondern verfeinern sie mit allerlei internationalen Einflüssen. Serviert wird dieser Genuss gern in höheren Etagen mit Blick auf die Stadt und deren weltberühmtes Symbol, den Eiffelturm. So zum Beispiel im futuristischen „Georges" im oberen Stock des Centre Pompidou oder im „Maison Blanche" nahe der Champs-Elysées.

Vorher kann man in den großen Kaufhäusern aus dem 19. Jahrhundert, dem „Printemps" oder den „Galeries Lafayette", einkaufen und dabei die prächtigen Jugendstil-Glaskuppeln bewundern. Eine ganz andere Art des Pariser Chic bieten Vintage-Läden wie „Espace Kiliwatch" und „Wochdom", die zu ausgiebigem Stöbern einladen.

Auf jeden Fall sollte man es zwischendurch nicht versäumen, im Jardin du Luxembourg oder auf der Place des Vosges im szenigen Marais-Viertel zu sitzen, um das Pariser Savoir-vivre zu genießen.

Elke Buscher

Introduction

Paris, cette ville de renommée mondiale sur les bords de la Seine, mérite bien sa réputation. Depuis plus de 100 ans, Paris est considéré comme la métropole européenne de l'Art. De nombreux musées en témoignent, qu'ils soient logés dans des palais historiques ou dans des édifices modernes conçus spécialement pour servir l'Art.

Outre la culture et l'art français, vous pouvez, dans certains musées, aussi découvrir la cuisine française, qui a également contribué à la réputation de Paris, par exemple au « Café de l'Homme » dans le Palais Chaillot ou au « Café Marly » au Louvre, le plus grand musée du monde. Des chefs récompensés par plusieurs étoiles se précipitent en grand nombre à Paris et, depuis longtemps, ne se contentent plus de la cuisine française, mais l'affinent de toutes sortes d'influences étrangères. Ces plaisirs seront volontiers servis aux étages supérieurs d'où vous pourrez contempler la ville et son symbole universellement connu, la Tour Eiffel. C'est le cas dans le futuriste « Georges » situé au sixième étage du Centre Pompidou ou à la « Maison Blanche », près des Champs-Elysées.

Vous aurez pu précédemment faire des achats dans les grands magasins datant du 19ème siècle comme le « Printemps » ou les « Galeries Lafayette » tout en contemplant les somptueuses coupoles de verre style Art nouveau. C'est, par contre, un tout autre genre de chic que proposent les magasins vintage comme « l'Espace Kiliwatch » et « Wochdom » en vous invitant à une fouille intensive.

En aucun cas, vous ne manquerez d'aller vous asseoir dans le Jardin du Luxembourg ou sur la Place des Vosges située dans le quartier bouillonnant du Marais, afin de pouvoir goûter au savoir-vivre parisien.

Elke Buscher

Introducción

París hace honor a su reputación como metrópoli a orillas del Sena, ya que desde hace más de cien años está considerada la capital europea del arte. La mejor prueba de ello son sus numerosos museos, alojados en históricos palacios o en modernos edificios concebidos con un único fin: el arte.

Hoy en día es posible descubrir en algunos de esos museos no sólo el arte y la cultura franceses, sino también su cocina, la cual ha contribuido de manera determinante en dar fama mundial a esta gran ciudad. Buena muestra de ello son el "Café de l'Homme" en el Palacio de Chaillot, o el "Café Marly" en el Museo del Louvre, el museo más grande del mundo. Los cocineros estrella han tomado literalmente en masa la capital gala, añadiendo a la cocina tradicional francesa multitud de influencias internacionales. Los apetitosos platos se sirven preferentemente en los pisos superiores con vistas a la ciudad y a su mundialmente famoso símbolo, la Torre Eiffel. Un buen ejemplo es el restaurante futurista "Georges" en el piso superior del Centro Pompidou, como también lo es el "Maison Blanche" cerca de los Campos Elíseos.

Antes de almorzar se puede ir de compras a los vastos almacenes del siglo XIX, el "Printemps" o las "Galeries Lafayette", y admirar las espléndidas cúpulas de cristal de estilo modernista. Las tiendas vintage, como "Espace Kiliwatch" y "Wochdom", ofrecen otra forma del chic parisino e invitan a pasar horas rebuscando entre sus artículos.

No puede faltar una parada en el Jardín del Luxemburgo o en la Plaza de los Vosgos del popular barrio de Marais para gozar del estilo de vida parisino.

Elke Buscher

RESTAURANTS & CAFÉS

Baccarat

11, place des Etats-Unis
75116 Paris
16e Arrondissement
Phone: +33 / 1 / 40 22 11 10
www.baccarat.fr

Opening hours: Mon–Sat 12.15 pm to 2.15 pm and 7.15 pm to 10.15 pm
Prices: €€€€
Cuisine: International, changes with season
Public transportation: Métro 6 Boissiere, 9 Iéna
Map: No. 1

Situated on the first floor of the Baccarat building, where Marie-Laure de Noailles used to dine, and surrounded by magnificent halls, the Cristal Room invites us to spend some time and relax. Philippe Starck has managed to preserve the room's original charm and elegance and to skillfully combine it with modern elements. Exposed bricks are framed with paneling and gold ornaments, creating a backdrop of extreme cultivation where guests can enjoy culinary pampering.

Im ersten Stock des Hauses Baccarat, wo seinerzeit Marie-Laure de Noailles zu speisen pflegte, lädt der von prunkvollen Sälen umgebene Cristal Room zum Verweilen ein. Philippe Starck ist es gelungen, den ursprünglichen Charme und die Klasse des Raumes zu bewahren und gekonnt mit modernen Elementen zu kombinieren. Unverputzte Ziegelsteine werden von Vertäfelungen und Goldverzierungen umschlossen und bilden eine Kulisse höchster Kultiviertheit, in der sich Besucher kulinarisch verwöhnen lassen können.

Au cœur des fastueux salons du premier étage de la Maison Baccarat, la Cristal Room, véritable espace de vie, est située dans l'ancienne salle à manger de Marie-Laure de Noailles. Philippe Starck a su en conserver le chic originel et la classe, tout en la dotant d'une empreinte de modernité : on s'y restaure ou se désaltère dans un décor, sophistication extrême, de briques brutes enchâssées de lambris et dorures.

Rodeado de suntuosas salas, el restaurante Cristal Room en la primera planta de la casa Baccarat invita a quedarse un rato. Se encuentra justo donde Marie-Laure de Noailles tuviera antaño su comedor. Philippe Starck ha conseguido mantener el encanto y la clase originales de la habitación, conjugándolos a la perfección con elementos modernos. Las paredes de ladrillo caravista, revestidas de paneles de madera y ornamentos dorados, crean un escenario de gran refinamiento, en el que los visitantes pueden degustar los mayores placeres culinarios.

Barlotti

35, place du Marché Saint-Honoré
75001 Paris
1er Arrondissement
Phone: +33 / 1 / 44 86 97 97
www.barlotti.fr

Opening hours: Daily noon to 2 am
Prices: €€€
Cuisine: Italian
Public transportation: Métro 1 Tuileries; 7, 14 Pyramides
Map: No. 2

Lydia Hearst's Special Tip
This Italian restaurant has a wonderfully chic atmosphere and is especially great for Sunday brunch.

On three floors, Barlotti cultivates an absolute passion for Italy and Italian cuisine. The specialty of the house is risotto, offered in several variations. In front of stone walls and large paintings inspired by the work of Gustav Klimt, this is how to enjoy *dolce vita* in Paris.

Das Barlotti kultiviert auf drei Stockwerken eine richtiggehende Leidenschaft für Italien und seine Gastronomie. Die Spezialität des Hauses ist das Risotto, das gleich in mehreren Variationen angeboten wird. Vor steinernen Wänden und großen Gemälden, die vom Werk Gustav Klimts inspiriert sind, lässt sich so auch in Paris das Dolce Vita genießen.

Le Barlotti cultive sur trois étages une véritable passion pour l'Italie et sa gastronomie. La spécialité de la maison, le risotto, est servi sous diverses variantes. Devant des murs en pierres et des grands tableaux inspirés de l'œuvre de Gustav Klimt, vous pourrez vivre, aussi à Paris, la Dolce Vita.

En sus tres pisos, el restaurante Barlotti cultiva una auténtica pasión hacia Italia y su gastronomía. La especialidad de la casa es el risotto, el cual se sirve en diferentes variaciones. Rodeado de paredes de piedra y grandes cuadros inspirados en la obra de Gustav Klimt, es posible disfrutar la dolce vita también en París.

Restaurant BON

25, rue de la Pompe
75116 Paris
16e Arrondissement
Phone: +33 / 1 / 40 72 70 00
www.restaurantbon.fr

Opening hours: Daily noon to 2 pm and 7:30 pm to midnight
Prices: €€
Cuisine: International-Asian fusion
Public transportation: Métro 9 Rue de la Pompe
Map: No. 3

BON is one of the first restaurants in Paris designed by Philippe Starck. During the remodel, too, the master himself pitched in with the work. He combines simple black and white with highly ornate furniture, and a black rhinoceros head on the wall serves as a special eye-catcher. The cuisine is every bit as creative as the decor: primarily Asian-inspired light fusion dishes are served in addition to such classics as *foie gras*.

Das BON gehört zu den ersten von Philippe Starck entworfenen Restaurants in Paris. Auch bei seiner Neugestaltung hat der Meister selbst Hand angelegt. Schlichtes Schwarz-Weiß kombiniert er hier mit äußerst verschnörkeltem Mobiliar, und als besonderer Blickfang dient ein schwarzer Rhinozeroskopf an der Wand. Genauso kreativ wie die Einrichtung ist die Küche, denn neben Klassikern wie Foie Gras werden vor allem asiatisch inspirierte leichte Fusion-Gerichte serviert.

Parmi les tous premiers restaurants parisiens a avoir été décoré par Philippe Starck, BON vient d'être relooké par le maître lui-meme. L'élégance du noir et blanc est ici combinée à un mobilier particulièrement baroque tandis qu'au mur, une tête noire de rhinocéros capte les regards. À l'image de la décoration, la cuisine est tout aussi créative : à coté de classiques comme le foie gras, vous sont servis des plats « fusion », surtout d'inspiration asiatique.

El BON es uno de los primeros restaurantes diseñados por Philippe Starck en París. El propio Starck ha colaborado en la renovación del local, combinando simples blancos y negros con un mobiliario colmado de arabescos. El centro de atención es una cabeza de rinoceronte negro que cuelga de la pared. Tan creativa como la decoración es su cocina, ya que junto a los clásicos como el foie gras se sirven sobre todo platos de cocina de fusión de inspiración asiática.

Costes

239, rue Saint-Honoré
75001 Paris
1er Arrondissement
Phone: +33 / 1 / 42 44 50 00
www.hotelcostes.com

Opening hours: Daily 7 am to 2 am
Prices: €€€
Cuisine: Classical
Public transportation: Métro 1, 8, 12 Concorde   **Map:** No. 4

Lydia Hearst's Special Tip
This place is extremely romantic and filled with chic clientele, an elegant wait staff and dining by candlelight in an open-air courtyard in the center of the Hotel Costes.

The style of Napoleon the Third dominates the interior of the restaurant of Hotel Costes, which for many years has been the de rigueur meeting point of the rich and beautiful—especially after an extended shopping trip down the luxurious Rue Saint-Honoré. The restaurant stands out for its elegance, attentive service, and the classic French cuisine that is also served in the attractive courtyard.

Der Stil Napoleons des Dritten bestimmt das Innere des Restaurants des Hotels Costes, das schon seit vielen Jahren unverzichtbarer Treffpunkt der Reichen und Schönen ist – vor allem nach einem ausgedehnten Shopping-Bummel auf der luxuriösen Rue Saint-Honoré. Das Restaurant besticht durch seine Eleganz, einen aufmerksamen Service und die klassische französische Küche, die gerne auch im hübschen Hof serviert wird.

Le style Napoléon III marque l'intérieur du restaurant de l'Hôtel Costes, qui, depuis de nombreuses années est le point de rencontre incontournable des personnes du beau monde – surtout après un tour de magasins dans la luxueuse rue Saint-Honoré. Le restaurant séduit par son élégance, son service impeccable et sa cuisine française traditionnelle que vous pouvez aussi vous faire servir dans le patio.

El estilo de Napoleón III caracteriza el interior del restaurante del hotel Costes, cita obligada de ricos y famosos desde hace muchos años, quienes suelen llegar aquí tras un largo recorrido por las tiendas de la lujosa Rue Saint Honoré. El restaurante sobresale por su elegancia, por su atento servicio y por sus platos de cocina francesa clásica, los cuales pueden ser degustados también en el precioso patio.

Café de Flore

172, boulevard Saint-Germain
75006 Paris
6e Arrondissement
Phone: +33 / 1 / 45 48 55 26
www.cafe-de-flore.com

Opening hours: Daily 7 am to 1:30 am
Prices: €
Cuisine: Traditional French
Public transportation: Métro 4 Saint-Germain-des-Prés   **Map:** No. 5

Lydia Hearst's Special Tip
One of the most famous cafés in the world. Through generations, Picasso and other artists frequented this spot. Often filled with famous patrons, it is recently filled with tourists.

One of the most venerable cafés in the Saint-Germain-des-Prés area is Café de Flore from the 19th century, where Jean-Paul Sartre and Simone de Beauvoir used to spend hours working on their manuscripts. The terrace is an ideal location to observe the comings and goings on the Boulevard Saint-Germain. Regulars and celebrities, however, tend to sit on the discreet upper level.

Eines der traditionsreichen Cafés im Viertel Saint-Germain-des-Prés ist das Café de Flore aus dem 19. Jahrhundert, in dem Jean-Paul Sartre und Simone de Beauvoir seinerzeit stundenlang an ihren Manuskripten feilten. Die Terrasse ist ein idealer Platz, um das Treiben auf dem Boulevard Saint-Germain zu beobachten. Stammkunden und bekannte Gesichter setzen sich jedoch eher in das diskrete obere Stockwerk.

Datant du 19ème siècle, le Café de Flore fait partie des cafés à la longue tradition du quartier de Saint-Germain-des-Prés. C'est ici que Jean-Paul Sartre et Simone de Beauvoir travaillaient pendant des heures sur leurs manuscrits. La terrasse est l'endroit idéal pour observer le tumulte du boulevard Saint-Germain. Les habitués et les célébrités s'assoient plutôt à l'étage supérieur, plus discret.

Uno de los cafés con más tradición del barrio de Saint-Germain-des-Prés es el Café de Flore del siglo XIX, en el que en otro tiempo Jean-Paul Sartre y Simone de Beauvoir pasaron horas retocando sus manuscritos. La terraza es el lugar ideal para observar el ir y venir en el bulevar Saint-Germain. Los clientes habituales y las caras conocidas prefieren sin embargo la intimidad del piso superior.

Café de l'Homme

17, place du Trocadéro
75116 Paris
16e Arrondissement
Phone: +33 / 1 / 44 05 30 15
www.lecafedelhomme.com

Opening hours: Daily noon to 2 am
Prices: €€
Cuisine: Modern and traditional
Public transportation: Métro 6, 9 Trocadéro
Map: No. 6

Decorated in the art deco style, Café de l'Homme, the restaurant of the ethnological museum at the Palais de Chaillot, offers a magnificent view both inside and out of the Eiffel Tower and the Seine. During the day you can simply enjoy the view over a drink or small snack. In the evening a menu is served in which guests can choose between traditional French and international dishes.

Das im Art-déco-Stil eingerichtete Café de l'Homme, Restaurant des Völkerkundemuseums im Palais de Chaillot, bietet innen wie außen einen prächtigen Blick auf den Eiffelturm und die Seine. Tagsüber genießt man einfach bei einem Getränk oder einem kleinen Snack die Aussicht, abends wird ein Menü serviert, bei dem die Gäste zwischen traditionell französischen oder internationalen Gerichten wählen können.

Le Café de l'Homme au style Art déco, restaurant du Musée de l'Homme dans le Palais de Chaillot, offre, à l'extérieur comme à l'intérieur, une vue somptueuse sur la Tour Eiffel et la Seine. Pendant la journée, vous pouvez simplement profiter de la vue en prenant un verre ou un petit en-cas. Le soir, on vous propose un menu dans lequel les invités peuvent choisir entre de la cuisine française et des plats internationaux.

Decorado en estilo *art déco*, el restaurante Café de l'Homme del museo etnológico del Palais de Chaillot ofrece a sus visitantes unas impresionantes vistas de la torre Eiffel y del Sena, tanto desde dentro del establecimiento como desde su terraza. Durante el día se puede disfrutar del panorama junto a una bebida o un pequeño snack. Por la noche se sirve un menú que permite a los clientes elegir entre los platos tradicionales franceses y los platos internacionales.

Café Marly

Cour Napoléon
93, rue de Rivoli
75001 Paris
1er Arrondissement
Phone: +33 / 1 / 49 26 06 60

Opening hours: Daily 8 am to 2 am
Prices: €€
Cuisine: French
Public transportation: Métro 1, 7 Palais Royal — Musée du Louvre
Map: No. 7

Café Marly is located in the Richelieu Wing of the Louvre. From the terrace you can enjoy an outstanding view of the glass pyramid. But the interior is worth a visit, as well. Seemingly far from the hubbub of the tourist masses, you can let yourself sink into soft velvet chairs in tasteful surroundings. Inside and outside, international dishes are served in addition to scrumptious cakes and tortes.

Im Richelieu-Flügel des Louvre ist das Café Marly untergebracht, von dessen Terrasse man einen vortrefflichen Blick auf die gläserne Pyramide genießt. Doch auch das Innere lohnt einen Aufenthalt. Scheinbar weit vom Trubel der Touristenströme kann man sich in stilvollem Dekor in weiche Samtsessel sinken lassen. Innen wie außen werden neben köstlichen Kuchen und Torten auch internationale Gerichte serviert.

Le Café Marly se trouve dans l'aile Richelieu du Louvre et, de sa terrasse, vous profitez d'une superbe vue sur la pyramide en verre. Par ailleurs, même l'intérieur vaut le détour. Dans un décor de style et apparemment à mille lieux du tumulte et des flots de touristes, vous vous enfoncez dans des canapés moelleux en velours. À l'intérieur comme à l'extérieur, vous est servi, à coté de délicieux gâteaux et tartes, des plats internationaux.

El Café Marly se sitúa en el ala Richelieu del Museo del Louvre y su terraza permite disfrutar de una excelente vista de la pirámide de cristal. Pero el interior también merece una visita. Aparentemente alejado del bullicio de los turistas, uno puede hundirse en una mullida butaca de terciopelo rodeado de una elegante decoración. Tanto en el interior como en el exterior se sirven exquisitos pasteles y tartas, además de platos internacionales.

Georges

Centre Georges Pompidou, 6th floor
19, rue Beaubourg
75004 Paris
4e Arrondissement
Phone: +33 / 1 / 44 78 47 99
www.centrepompidou.fr

Opening hours: Wed–Mon 10:30 am to 2 am
Prices: €€€
Cuisine: Modern
Public transportation: Métro 1, 4, 7, 11, 14 Châtelet
Map: No. 8

Utility pipes in different colors form the outline for the futuristic Restaurant Georges on the sixth floor of the Centre Pompidou cultural center. It features innovative international dishes and dining on the terrace if the weather is good. But guests do not come only for the light fare: the view over the city's rooftops—by day and by night—is also worth a visit.

Versorgungsrohre in verschiedenen Farben bilden den Rahmen für das futuristisch gestaltete Restaurant Georges in der sechsten Etage des Kulturzentrums Centre Pompidou. Es serviert – bei gutem Wetter auch auf der Terrasse – innovative internationale Gerichte. Doch die Gäste kommen nicht nur wegen der leichten Küche; der Blick über die Dächer der Stadt, bei Tag wie bei Nacht, ist ebenso lohnend.

Des tuyaux d'alimentation de couleurs différentes constituent le cadre du Georges, restaurant à la conception futuriste, qui se situe au sixième étage du centre culturel Pompidou. Il sert une cuisine internationale innovatrice – par beau temps, aussi sur la terrasse. Cependant, les visiteurs ne viennent pas seulement pour déguster sa cuisine légère : la vue sur les toits de la ville, de jour comme de nuit, vaut également le détour.

El restaurante Georges se encuentra en la sexta planta del Centro Pompidou. Los tubos de abastecimiento de diferentes colores y la cubierta de aluminio le dan un aspecto realmente futurista. La carta ofrece platos internacionales innovadores que, con buen tiempo, se pueden disfrutar también en la terraza. No obstante, los clientes no vienen sólo por la cocina ligera: el panorama sobre los tejados de la ciudad también merece la pena, tanto de día como de noche.

Ginger

11, rue de la Trémoille
75008 Paris
8e Arrondissement
Phone: +33 / 1 / 47 23 37 32

Opening hours: Daily noon to 2 am
Prices: €€€
Cuisine: Asian
Public transportation: Métro 1 George V
Map: No. 9

Ginger is the venue for aficionados of Asian cuisine. The Cambodian chef draws his inspiration from Cambodia, Laos, and Vietnam, playing with spices and developing unusual dishes such as spring rolls with lobster and mango or gilt-head bream in banana leaves. Service is excellent and so friendly that you'll hate to leave.

Der Treffpunkt für Liebhaber der asiatischen Küche ist das Ginger. Der Küchenchef, selbst kambodschanischen Ursprungs, lässt sich von Ideen aus Kambodscha, Laos oder Vietnam inspirieren, spielt mit Gewürzen und entwickelt ungewöhnliche Gerichte wie Frühlingsrollen mit Hummer und Mango oder Dorade in Bananenblättern. Der Service ist vorzüglich und so freundlich, dass man ungern wieder geht.

Le Ginger est le point de rencontre des amoureux de la cuisine asiatique. Le chef, d'origine cambodgienne, s'inspire d'idées provenant du Cambodge, du Laos ou du Vietnam, joue avec les épices et développe des plats inhabituels comme des rouleaux de printemps au homard et à la mangue ou de la dorade dans des feuilles de banane. Le service est impeccable et l'accueil si sympathique qu'il est difficile de s'en aller.

El Ginger es el lugar de encuentro para los amantes de la cocina asiática. De origen camboyano, el cocinero jefe se inspira en ideas sacadas de las gastronomías camboyana, laosiana y vietnamita, juega con las especias y crea platos insólitos, como los rollitos de primavera con langosta y mango o la dorada en hojas de plátano. El servicio es exquisito y muy agradable, tanto que da verdadera pena marcharse.

GINGER

Kong

1, rue du Pont Neuf
75001 Paris
1er Arrondissement
Phone: +33 / 1 / 40 39 09 00
www.kong.fr

Opening hours: Daily 10:30 am to 2 am
Prices: €€€
Cuisine: French-asian fusion
Public transportation: Métro 7 Pont Neuf   **Map:** No. 10

Lydia Hearst's Special Tip
Philippe Starck is the mastermind behind the stunning decor. This place is trendy and cutting-edge with a fabulous view overlooking the river Seine. Kong is famously recognized for being in the finale of hit television series Sex and the City.

On the eighth floor of the Kenzo Building, Kong has found its place as an absolutely "in" spot. Designed by Philippe Starck, its chairs are inspired by mangas; you sit in them beneath a glass cupola with a view of the Seine and Pont Neuf, before storming the dance floor on the lower level. The food is served so quickly that you have to hurry to enjoy the view.

Im achten Stock des Kenzo-Gebäudes hat sich das Kong als absoluter In-Treff etabliert. Von Philippe Starck entworfen, sitzt man auf seinen von Mangas inspirierten Stühlen unter einer Glaskuppel und blickt auf die Seine und Pont Neuf, bevor man im unteren Stock auf die Tanzfläche stürmen kann. Das Essen wird allerdings so flott serviert, dass man sich mit dem Genießen der Aussicht beeilen muss.

Au huitième étage de l'immeuble Kenzo, le Kong, conçu par Philippe Starck, est devenu le point de rencontre absolument tendance. Asseyez-vous sur ses chaises inspirées des mangas en dessous d'une voûte en verre tout en plongeant votre regard sur la Seine et le Pont-Neuf, avant de descendre à l'étage inférieur et vous déchainer sur la piste de danse. Par contre, les plats sont servis si rapidement qu'il faut se dépêcher de profiter de la vue.

Alojado en el octavo piso del edificio Kenzo, el Kong, diseñado por Philippe Starck, se ha consolidado como uno de los locales más de moda. Sus sillas inspiradas en el cómic manga se sitúan bajo una cúpula de cristal, desde donde se puede divisar el Sena y el Puente Nuevo antes de saltar a la pista de baile. Sin embargo, la comida se sirve con tanta rapidez que hay que apresurarse en disfrutar de la vista.

La Cantine du Faubourg

105, rue du Faubourg Saint-Honoré
75008 Paris
8e Arrondissement
Phone: +33 / 1 / 42 56 22 22
www.lacantine.com

Opening hours: Daily 11 am to 4 am
Prices: €€€
Cuisine: International
Public transportation: Métro 9 Saint-Philippe-du-Roule
Map: No. 11

Glamorous, chic and always in, that's La Cantine du Faubourg. Huge screens on the walls and a sophisticated lighting control system skillfully set the stage each hour in the locale; there are also regular exhibitions which additionally beautify the space. And yet the cuisine does not suffer: creatively refined French classics like *pot-au-feu* and tuna steak taste marvelous.

Glamourös, schick und immer angesagt ist das La Cantine du Faubourg. Riesige Bildschirme an den Wänden und eine ausgeklügelte Lichtregie setzen das Lokal zu jeder Stunde gekonnt in Szene; außerdem finden regelmäßig Ausstellungen statt, die das Lokal zusätzlich verschönern. Die Küche leidet nicht darunter: kreativ verfeinerte französische Klassiker wie Pot-au-feu oder Thunfischsteak schmecken vorzüglich.

La Cantine du Faubourg est glamour, chic et toujours tendance. Des immenses écrans aux murs et un astucieux éclairage composent l'habile mise en scène de ce restaurant, et ce, à toute heure. Par ailleurs, des expositions y sont régulièrement logées et se chargent d'embellir encore davantage le lieu. La cuisine n'en pâtit pas : vous pourrez vous délecter de classiques français comme le pot-au-feu ou le steak au thon, affinés d'une dose de créativité.

Glamorosa, elegante y muy de moda: así es La Cantine du Faubourg. Enormes pantallas en las paredes y una iluminación muy ingeniosa disponen a cualquier hora el escenario ideal. Además, se celebran regularmente exposiciones que embellecen el local aún más si cabe. La cocina no se resiente en absoluto: Los clásicos franceses como el *pot au feu* o el filete de atún son mejorados con un toque creativo, consiguiendo un sabor exquisito.

Le Saut du Loup

107, rue de Rivoli
75001 Paris
1er Arrondissement
Phone: +33 / 1 / 42 25 49 55
www.lesautduloup.com

Opening hours: Daily noon to 2 am
Prices: €€€
Cuisine: French
Public transportation: Métro 1, 7 Palais Royal – Musée du Louvre   **Map:** No. 12

Lydia Hearst's Special Tip
The place to sit is by the window, with a view of the Tuileries Gardens. The restaurant is characterized by its purity of line and minimalist style and very light atmosphere.

In the middle of the applied-arts museum we find Le Saut du Loup. Its minimalist industrial chic in black-and-white contrasts with the historical surroundings, the Louvre and the Tuileries are just a stone's throw away, so it's natural on nice afternoons to take a break with tea and pastry on the terrace. Creative French cuisine is served for lunch and dinner.

Mitten im Kunstgewerbemuseum liegt das Le Saut du Loup. Sein minimalistischer Industrie-Chic in Schwarz-Weiß kontrastiert mit der historischen Umgebung, denn der Louvre und die Tuilerien sind nur einen Katzensprung entfernt. An schönen Nachmittagen bietet sich deshalb eine Pause bei Tee und Patisserie auf der Terrasse an; mittags wie abends wird kreative französische Küche serviert.

Le Saut du Loup se trouve au cœur du Musée des Arts Décoratifs. Son chic minimaliste industriel en noir et blanc contraste avec les environs empreints d'histoire du Louvre et des Tuileries qui sont à deux pas. C'est pourquoi l'après-midi, par beau temps, la terrasse invite à une pause autour d'un thé accompagné de pâtisseries ; le midi, tout comme le soir, on y sert une cuisine française créative.

El Le Saut du Loup se ubica en pleno Museo de las Artes Decorativas. Su estilo chic minimalista industrial en blanco y negro contrasta con el histórico entorno, ya que el Museo del Louvre y los Jardines de las Tullerías están a tan sólo unos pasos. En las tardes soleadas la terraza invita a disfrutar de una taza de té y unas pastas. Tanto al mediodía como por la noche se sirve cocina creativa francesa.

Le Train Bleu

Gare de Lyon, Place Louis-Armand
75012 Paris
12e Arrondissement
Phone: +33 / 1 / 43 43 09 06
www.le-train-bleu.com

Opening hours: Daily 11:30 am to 3 pm and 7 pm to 11 pm
Prices: €€€
Cuisine: Traditional French
Public transportation: Métro 1, 14 Gare de Lyon; RER A, D Gare de Lyon   **Map:** No. 13

Russell James' Special Tip
Despite the train-station locale, this classic stunner decorated with mosaics and murals remains unmatched.

Le Train Bleu is anything but an ordinary train station restaurant. Located on the first level of the Gare de Lyon, the belle epoque shines here in its most beautiful radiance. Paintings by famous artists of that period decorate the ceilings and walls, inviting us to forget the hubbub of the station. Culinarily, the restaurant is strongly oriented to traditional Lyonnais cuisine—in concord with the name of the station.

Das Le Train Bleu ist alles andere als ein gewöhnliches Bahnhofsrestaurant. Im ersten Stock des Gare de Lyon gelegen, erstrahlt die Belle Epoque hier in ihrem schönsten Glanz. Gemälde berühmter Künstler jener Zeit schmücken Decke und Wände und lassen den Trubel des Bahnhofs vergessen. Kulinarisch orientiert sich das Restaurant – dem Namen des Bahnhofs entsprechend – stark an der traditionellen Lyoner Küche.

Le Train Bleu est tout sauf un restaurant ordinaire de gare. Situé au premier étage de la gare de Lyon, la Belle Epoque brille ici de son plus bel éclat. Des peintures de célèbres artistes de cette époque ornent plafonds et murs et font oublier le tumulte de la gare. L'art culinaire du restaurant s'inspire fortement, à l'image du nom de la gare, de la cuisine lyonnaise traditionnelle.

Le Train Bleu no tiene nada que ver con los habituales restaurantes de estación ferroviaria. El local se halla en el primer piso de la estación Gare de Lyon, y la *belle époque* brilla aquí con todo su esplendor. El techo y las paredes están adornados con pinturas de famosos artistas de la época que sumergen el barullo de los viajeros en el olvido. Como indica el nombre de la estación, la cocina del restaurante se centra principalmente en los platos tradicionales lioneses.

Maison Blanche

15, avenue Montaigne
75008 Paris
8e Arrondissement
Phone: +33 / 1 / 47 23 55 99
www.maison-blanche.fr

Opening hours: Mon–Thu noon to 2 pm and 8 pm to 11 pm, Fri–Sat 8 pm to 11 pm
Prices: €€€€
Cuisine: French
Public transportation: Métro 1 Franklin D. Roosevelt; 9 Alma Marceau
Map: No. 14

This unique gem of French elegance floats like a bridge over the roofs of the Théâtre des Champs-Elysées on Avenue Montaigne, thrilling its guests with a spectacular view of Paris. Inspired by the passion of the Pourcel twins, chef Thierry Vaissière has made Maison Blanche into a locus of true culinary revolution.

Wie eine Brücke spannt sich dieses einzigartige Schmuckstück französischer Eleganz über die Dächer des Théâtre des Champs-Elysées an der Avenue Montaigne und begeistert seine Gäste mit einer traumhaften Sicht über Paris. Inspiriert von der Leidenschaft der Zwillingsbrüder Pourcel, hat Küchenchef Thierry Vaissière die Maison Blanche zu einem Ort wahrer kulinarischer Revolution werden lassen.

Tel un pont suspendu au-dessus du Théâtre des Champs-Elysées, sur l'avenue Montaigne, ce haut lieu de l'élégance française est un écrin privilégié offrant une vue époustouflante sur Paris. Thierry Vaissière, le chef, s'est inspiré de la passion jumelée des frères Pourcel pour faire de Maison Blanche le décor d'une véritable révolution culinaire.

Esta inigualable joya de la elegancia francesa parece estar suspendida sobre los tejados del Teatro de los Campos Elíseos en la avenida Montaigne, entusiasmando a sus invitados con una espectacular panorámica de París. Inspirado por la pasión de los gemelos Pourcel, el cocinero jefe Thierry Vaissière ha hecho del Maison Blanche un lugar de verdadera revolución culinaria.

Market

15, avenue Matignon
75008 Paris
8e Arrondissement
Phone: +33 / 1 / 56 43 40 90
www.jean-georges.com

Opening hours: Breakfast: Mon–Fri 8 am to 11 am; Lunch: Mon–Fri noon to 3 pm;
Dinner: Mon–Sun 7 pm to 11.30 pm; Brunch: Sat–Sun noon to 4.30 pm
Prices: €€
Cuisine: World fusion
Public transportation: Métro 1, 9 Franklin D. Roosevelt
Map: No. 15

Not far from the Champs-Elysées, Alsatian star chef Jean-Georges Vongerichten has opened Market.
There he remains true to his internationally successful culinary style combining seasonal French cuisine
with Italian or Asian elements. Lemongrass, ginger and sesame, the ingredients are not new, but newly
combined and therefore surprising time and again.

Unweit der Champs-Elysées hat der elsässische Starkoch Jean-Georges Vongerichten das Market eröffnet, in dem er kulinarisch seinem weltweit erfolgreichen Stil treu bleibt: Saisonale französische Küche
kombiniert er mit Elementen aus der italienischen oder asiatischen Küche. Zitronengras, Ingwer und
Sesam – alles nicht neu, aber doch neu zusammengestellt und deshalb immer wieder überraschend.

C'est non loin des Champs-Élysées que la star Jean-Georges Vongerichten, chef alsacien, a ouvert
le Market, où il reste fidèle à son style de renommée mondiale qui consiste en la combinaison d'une
cuisine française de saison avec des éléments de cuisine italienne et asiatique. De la citronnelle, du
gingembre et du sésame – rien de nouveau, mais ces ingrédients sont toutefois mariés d'une façon
innovatrice et donnent ainsi un résultat toujours surprenant.

No muy lejos de los Campos Elíseos, el cocinero estrella alsaciano Jean-Georges Vongerichten ha
abierto el Market. En este local el chef se mantiene, en lo culinario, fiel a su mundialmente aclamado
estilo: cocina francesa de temporada combinada con elementos de las gastronomías italiana y asiática.
Caña de limón, jengibre y sésamo –nada nuevo, pero combinado de manera distinta y por eso mismo
sorprendente.

CLUBS, LOUNGES & BARS

Bar du Murano Resort Paris

13, boulevard du Temple
75003 Paris
3e Arrondissement
Phone: +33 / 1 / 42 71 20 00
www.muranoresort.com

Opening hours: Daily 7 am to 2 am
Prices: €€
Public transportation: Métro 8 Filles du Calvaire
Map: No. 16

Lydia Hearst's Special Tip
Located on the Ile de France the staff is helpful and charming. This flirty hotel bar is fresh and fun for young people looking for a casual cocktail, food and excellent service.

Like the design hotel of the same name, the bar of the Murano Resort has developed into a very popular location every evening. This is due not only to its central location in the trendy Marais district, but also to the tasteful avant-garde décor. It's best to come here for an extended aperitif before starting your tour through the clubs of Paris.

Ebenso wie das gleichnamige Designhotel ist auch die Bar des Murano Resort allabendlich zu einem starken Anziehungspunkt geworden. Das liegt nicht nur an ihrer zentralen Lage im szenigen Marais-Viertel, sondern auch an der stilvollen avantgardistischen Einrichtung. Hier kommt man am besten für einen ausgedehnten Aperitif her, bevor die Tour durch die Clubs von Paris beginnt.

Le bar du Murano Resort est devenu, tout comme l'hôtel du même nom, un fort point d'attraction le soir. Il doit cela non seulement à son emplacement central dans le quartier bouillonnant du Marais mais aussi à son aménagement avant-gardiste très stylé. On y vient de préférence pour un apéritif prolongé avant d'entamer la tournée des clubs parisiens.

Al igual que el hotel de diseño del mismo nombre, el bar del Murano Resort se convierte cada noche en un punto de gran atractivo. No sólo por su céntrica ubicación en el barrio de Marais, sino también por su elegante mobiliario vanguardista. Lo mejor es tomarse un largo aperitivo antes de comenzar el recorrido por los clubes de París.

Bar du Plaza

25, avenue Montaigne
75008 Paris
8e Arrondissement
Phone: +33 / 1 / 53 67 66 00
www.plaza-athenee-paris.com

Opening hours: Daily 6 pm to 2 am
Public transportation: Métro 9 Alma Marceau
Map: No. 17

Lydia Hearst's Special Tip

One of the flashiest bars in Paris. With two lounge areas and filled with hotel guests, locals and celebrities, this is a fabulous date place and spot to hang out with friends. Don't miss their custom cocktails and "classy" gelatin shots influenced by Americans. The seductive yet elegant ambiance will keep you coming back!

To really be with-it, have a drink at the bar of Plaza Athénée. The design lounge with the bar in the shape of a huge glowing ice cube is the meeting spot for *tout Paris*, who appreciate the unusual, refreshing cocktails. Large paintings adorn the walls in the back part of the bar. Their oversized frames serve as benches, so guests become part of the artwork.

Richtig im Trend liegt, wer an der Bar des Plaza Athénée ein Gläschen trinkt. Die Designbar mit dem Tresen in Form eines leuchtenden, riesigen Eiswürfels ist Treffpunkt von „Tout Paris", das die ungewöhnlichen und erfrischenden Cocktails zu schätzen weiß. Im hinteren Teil der Bar zieren große Gemälde die Wände. Deren überdimensionale Rahmen dienen als Sitzfläche, sodass die Gäste Teil des Kunstwerks werden.

Il n'est rien de plus tendance que d'aller boire un verre au bar du Plaza Athénée. Le bar design avec son comptoir en forme d'immense glaçon lumineux est le lieu de rencontre du « tout Paris » qui sait apprécier les cocktails rafraichissants et insolites. Dans la partie antérieure du bar, les murs sont ornés de grands tableaux. Leurs cadres surdimensionnés font office de sièges, si bien que les hôtes deviennent une partie de l'œuvre.

Quien desee estar a la moda debe detenerse en el bar del hotel Plaza Athénée para tomar una copa. Este bar de diseño, con su barra en forma de enorme cubito de hielo iluminado, es uno de los puntos de encuentro para los parisinos que saben apreciar los cócteles más extraordinarios y refrescantes. Las paredes de la parte posterior del bar están adornadas con grandes cuadros. Sus marcos sobredimensionados sirven como asientos, haciendo que los invitados pasen a formar parte de las obras de arte.

Barrio Latino

46/48, rue du Faubourg Saint-Antoine
75012 Paris
12e Arrondissement
Phone: +33 / 1 / 55 78 84 75
www.buddhabar.com

Opening hours: Daily noon to 4 am
Prices: €
Public transportation: Métro 1, 5 Bastille
Map: No. 18

Russell James' Special Tip

Tapas bars, thumping dance floors and a Latin restaurant round out this multistory ode to hedonistic excess.

Barrio Latino is a restaurant, tapas bar and discotheque all rolled into one. On four levels surrounding the landmark-protected stairway designed by Gustave Eiffel, the Latin American culture of enjoyment unfolds and Latin American rhythms sound throughout the establishment. Later on there's energetic dancing. By the way, resident DJ Carlos Campos is responsible for the popular Barrio Latino compilations.

Das Barrio Latino ist Restaurant, Tapas-Bar und Diskothek in einem. Auf vier Stockwerken rund um die von Gustave Eiffel entworfene denkmalgeschützte Treppe entfaltet sich die lateinamerikanische Genusskultur und durchs ganze Haus klingen lateinamerikanische Rhythmen. Zu späterer Stunde wird dann heftig getanzt. Resident-DJ Carlos Campos ist übrigens für die bekannten Barrio-Latino-Compilations verantwortlich.

Le Barrio Latino est à la fois un restaurant, un bar à tapas et une discothèque. La culture sensuelle de l'Amérique latine se déploie sur quatre étages autour de l'escalier conçu par Gustave Eiffel et classé monument historique et c'est tout l'édifice qui résonne de rythmes sud-américains. On y danse avec entrain jusqu'à des heures tardives. Par ailleurs, le DJ du club Carlos Campos est à l'origine des célèbres compilations Barrio Latino.

El Barrio Latino es restaurante, bar de tapas y discoteca, todo en uno. La cultura latinoamericana del placer se revela en sus cuatro plantas, conectadas por una espectacular escalera, obra de Gustave Eiffel y considerada monumento histórico protegido. Los ritmos latinos resuenan por toda la casa y, según avanza la noche, los bailes se vuelven cada vez más ardientes. Por cierto, el DJ residente, Carlos Campos, es el responsable de los conocidos recopilatorios Barrio Latino.

Black Calvados

40, rue Pierre 1er dc Serbie
75008 Paris
8e Arrondissement
Phone: +33 / 1 / 47 20 77 77
www.bc-paris.com

Opening hours: Lounge: Tue–Sat 10 pm to 2 am; Club: Tue–Sat 11 pm to 4 am
Public transportation: Métro 1 George V
Map: No. 19

Black parquet, black benches, black stainless steel, and only a restrained level of lighting make Black Calvados a shadowy, ultracool nightclub. Serge Gainsbourg even dedicated a song to the "BC" in the 70s, and following its reopening in 2006 the club is again well on its way toward cult status, especially when they play rock on Thursdays and everybody dances on the sofas.

Schwarzes Parkett, schwarze Bänke, schwarzer Edelstahl und dazu nur eine dezente Beleuchtung machen das Black Calvados zu einem düsteren und ultracoolen Nachtclub. Serge Gainsbourg widmete dem „BC" in den 70ern sogar ein Lied, und nach seiner Wiedereröffnung 2006 ist der Club erneut auf dem besten Weg, zum Kult zu werden – vor allem wenn donnerstags Rock gespielt wird und alle auf den Sofas tanzen.

Parquet noir, banquettes noires, acier affiné noir et éclairage décent font du Black Calvados un club de nuit ultra cool des plus sombres. Serge Gainsbourg a même dédié une chanson au « BC » dans les années soixante-dix. Par ailleurs, depuis sa réouverture en 2006, le club est bien parti pour redevenir un endroit culte – en particulier grâce à ses soirées du jeudi au cours desquelles l'on joue du rock et tout le monde danse sur les canapés.

Parquet negro, bancos negros, acero fino negro; todo esto, combinado con una iluminación bastante discreta, hace del Black Calvados un club nocturno oscuro y muy cool. En los 70, Serge Gainsbourg dedicó incluso un tema musical al "BC" y, tras su reapertura en 2006, el club va camino de convertirse de nuevo en un local de culto; sobre todo los jueves, cuando se inunda de rock y todos bailan sobre los sofás.

Culture Bière

65, avenue des Champs-Elysées
75008 Paris
8e Arrondissement
Phone: +33 / 1 / 42 56 88 88
www.culturebiere.com

Opening hours: Mon noon to midnight, Tue–Wed noon to 2 am, Thu–Sat noon to 5 am
Prices: €
Public transportation: Métro 1 Franklin D. Roosevelt
Map: No. 20

Russell James' Special Tip
Beer fans will love this emporium offering cool drafts and beer-based foods and, oddly, skin products.

An innovative concept and modern design lurk behind Culture Bière on the Champs-Elysées. A restaurant, a bar, a lounge, and a shop meld together over three floors around the subject of beer, offering a unique platform to beer culture. Relaxation, companionship and discovery: life and enjoyment are the focus here. If you don't care for the product of the brewer's art, you can select from all manner of other beverages.

Ein innovatives Konzept und ein modernes Design verbergen sich hinter Culture Bière auf den Champs-Elysées, wo auf drei Stockwerken ein Restaurant, eine Bar, eine Lounge und ein Geschäft rund ums Thema Bier miteinander verschmelzen und der Bierkultur eine einzigartige Plattform bieten. Entspannung, Geselligkeit und Entdeckung; Leben und Genuss werden hier großgeschrieben. Wer Gebrautes nicht mag, kann zwischen allerlei anderen Getränken wählen.

C'est tout un concept innovant et design qui se cache derrière l'établissement Culture Bière sur les Champs Elysées. Là, sur trois étages, sont réunis à la fois un restaurant, un bar, un lounge et une boutique offrant à la bière un espace unique d'expression. Détente, convivialité et découvertes sont les maitres mots de ce lieu de vie et d'envies. À ceux qui ne raffolent pas de cette boisson brassée, il leur est proposé de choisir entre toutes sortes d'autres boissons.

El Culture Bière en los Campos Elíseos oculta un concepto innovador y un moderno diseño. En sus tres plantas se funden un restaurante, un bar, un salón y una tienda dedicados a la cerveza que constituyen una plataforma única donde rendir culto a esta bebida. Relajarse, relacionarse y descubrir: en este local, la vida y el placer se escriben con mayúsculas. Para aquellos que no quieran cerveza hay una gran variedad de bebidas entre las que elegir.

Regine's

49/51, rue de Ponthieu
75008 Paris
8e Arrondissement
Phone: +33 / 1 / 43 59 21 13

Opening hours: Tue–Sat 11 pm to 5 am
Public transportation: Métro 1 George V
Map: No. 21

A true jewel in the Parisian nightlife, Regine's draws a predominantly French crowd so you can see how real French people celebrate—if they let you in, that is, since Regine's is officially a members' club. For that reason it's worthwhile to get there early. Inside, happy attendees are greeted by a mix of French and international pop and funk, as well as an energetic party atmosphere.

Ein wahres Juwel im Pariser Nachtleben ist das Regine's, denn es wird vorwiegend von Franzosen aufgesucht. So kann man erleben, wie echte Franzosen feiern – wenn man hineingelassen wird, denn offiziell ist das Regine's ein Members Club. Früh kommen zahlt sich deshalb aus. Innen erwartet die Glücklichen dann ein Mix aus französischem und internationalem Pop und Funk sowie ausgelassene Partystimmung.

Le Regine's est un vrai bijou de la vie nocturne parisienne. Il est vrai qu'il n'est fréquenté pratiquement que par des Français. C'est ici que vous pourrez voir comment les vrais Français font la fête – si vous avez la chance qu'on vous laisse entrer, car le Regine's est officiellement un club de membres. C'est pourquoi le fait d'arriver tôt peut payer. A l'intérieur, vous attendent un mélange de pop et de funk aussi bien français qu'international ainsi qu'une ambiance décontractée.

El club Regine's es una auténtica joya de la noche parisina, ya que está frecuentado sobre todo por franceses. De esta manera se puede experimentar en primera persona cómo se divierten los nativos; siempre y cuando se consiga entrar, ya que el Regine's es oficialmente sólo para socios. Por esta razón es importante llegar pronto. En el interior, los afortunados pueden disfrutar de una mezcla francesa e internacional de pop y funk y una relajada atmósfera festiva.

Le Sens

23, rue de Ponthieu
75008 Paris
8e Arrondissement
Phone: +33 / 1 / 42 25 95 00
www.sens-paris.com

Opening hours: Thu–Sat 11 pm to 5 am
Prices: €€€
Public transportation: Métro 1 George V
Map: No. 22

Just a few steps from the Champs-Elysées, Le Sens pulls the trend-conscious into the restaurant, bar, and private club. With confident style, materials such as leather and wood are combined here with minimalist design, and the open spaces are delimited with controlled lighting. Videos by contemporary artists adorn the white walls.

Nur wenige Schritte von den Champs-Elysées zieht Le Sens Trendbewusste in Restaurant, Bar und Privatclub. Stilsicher werden hier Materialien wie Leder und Holz mit minimalistischem Design kombiniert und die offenen Räume durch Lichtregie voneinander abgegrenzt. Videos von zeitgenössischen Künstlern zieren die weißen Wände.

À quelques pas des Champs-Elysées, Le Sens est à la fois un restaurant, un bar et un club privé qui attire une clientèle branchée. Ici, c'est avec style que des matériaux comme le cuir et le bois se marient à un design minimaliste et que les pièces ouvertes les unes sur les autres sont délimitées par des effets de lumière. Des vidéos d'artistes contemporains sont projetées sur les murs nus.

Le Sens se encuentra a pocos pasos de los Campos Elíseos y a su restaurante, bar y club privado acuden a menudo los adeptos a la moda. El interior está decorado con gran estilo, combinando materiales como el cuero y la madera con diseños minimalistas y delimitando las habitaciones abiertas mediante la iluminación. Las paredes de color blanco están decoradas con vídeos de artistas contemporáneos.

Showcase

Pont Alexandre III
Port des Champs-Elysées
75008 Paris
8e Arrondissement
Phone: +33 / 1 / 45 61 25 43
www.showcase.fr

Opening hours: Fri–Sat 10 pm to 5 am
Public transportation: Métro 8, 13 Invalides; RER C Invalides
Map: No. 23

Hidden in the vaulted arch beneath one of the most beautiful bridges in Paris, the Pont Alexandre III near the Champs-Elysées, we find Showcase. Originally intended to open its doors only for marketing and fashion events, now bands of young musicians play there every weekend, transforming Showcase into a party center with the tagline "Sous le pont."

Im Gewölbe einer der schönsten Brücken von Paris, dem Pont Alexandre III. unweit der Champs-Elysées, versteckt sich das Showcase. Ursprünglich sollte es nur für Marketing- und Fashion-Events seine Tore öffnen, doch inzwischen spielen dort jedes Wochenende Bands oder junge Musiker und verwandeln das Showcase unter dem Motto „Sous le pont" in ein Partyzentrum.

C'est sous la voûte d'un des plus beaux ponts de Paris, le pont Alexandre III, non loin des Champs-Elysées que se cache le Showcase. A l'origine, il était destiné à des évènements de mode ou des opérations marketing, mais entre-temps, des groupes ou des jeunes musiciens y jouent tous les weekends et transforment le Showcase en un lieu festif s'articulant autour de la thématique « sous le pont ».

El club Showcase se esconde bajo la bóveda de uno de los puentes más bellos de París, el Alejandro III cerca de los Campos Elíseos. Originalmente solo abría sus puertas con motivo de eventos de marketing y moda, pero ahora se convierte cada fin de semana en escenario de conciertos de grupos y jóvenes músicos que, con el lema "sous le pont", convierten el Showcase en una fiesta.

The Ice Kube by Grey Goose

1/5, passage Ruelle
75018 Paris
18e Arrondissement
Phone: +33 / 1 / 42 05 20 00
www.kubehotel.com

Opening hours: Wed–Sat 7 pm to 1:30 am, Sun 2 pm to 11 pm, reservation mandatory
Prices: 38 € / 30 min and 4 cocktails with Grey Goose vodka
Public transportation: Métro 2 La Chapelle
Map: No. 24

If you enjoy drinking cocktails at below-zero temperatures, The Ice Kube by Grey Goose is for you. Special Ice Kuber clothing provided by Puma is handed out at the entrance of the design hotel Kube. Visitors are first invited into an area kept at +40°F to become acclimated. They then proceed into Antarctic temperatures. Behind an ice curtain, a surreal and unique world and a cocktail tasting with Grey Goose vodka, of course, await the guests.

Wer seine Drinks gerne bei Minusgraden zu sich nimmt, ist in The Ice Kube by Grey Goose gut aufgehoben. Am Eingang des Designhotels Kube wird von Puma bereitgestellte spezielle Ice Kuber-Kleidung verteilt. Um sich zu akklimatisieren, werden die Besucher zunächst in einen +5 °C kalten Bereich gebeten. Und dann geht es ab in antarktische Temperaturen. Hinter einem Vorhang aus Eis warten eine surreale und einzigartige Welt sowie eine Cocktail-Verkostung – natürlich mit Grey Goose Wodka – auf die Gäste.

Si vous aimez boire un verre à moins de zérodegrés, The Ice Kube by Grey Goose est tout à fait ce qu'il vous faut. A votre arrivée à l'hôtel design Kube, une tenue spéciale Ice Kuber fournie par Puma vous est mise à disposition avant d'entrer dans le sas à +5 °C pour vous acclimater avant le grand frisson ! Derrière un rideau de glace, un environnement surréaliste et insolite vous attend de dégustation de cocktails à base de vodka Grey Goose.

Quien desee disfrutar de una copa a temperaturas bajo cero no encontrará mejor lugar que The Ice Kube by Grey Goose para hacerlo. En la entrada del hotel de diseño Kube se reparte ropa especialmente diseñada por Puma para los Ice Kubers. Para poder aclimatarse, los visitantes son llevados en primer lugar a una zona con una temperatura de +5 °C. Después les espera un frío polar. Tras una cortina de hielo aguarda un mundo surrealista y único, además de una degustación de cócteles; por supuesto, con vodka Grey Goose.

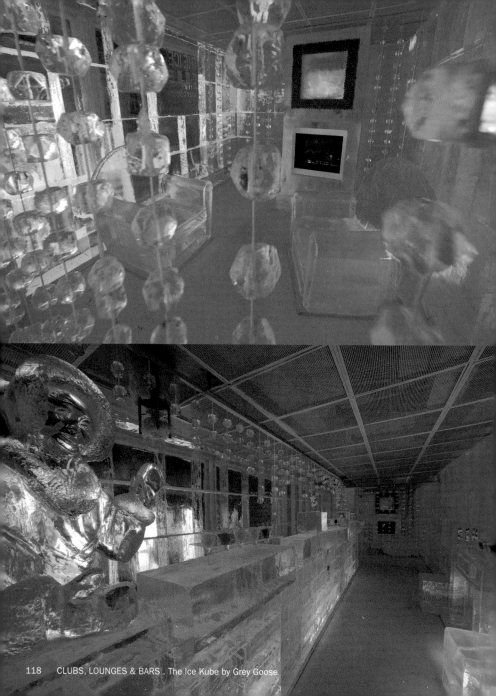

SHOPS

Colette

213, rue Saint-Honoré
75001 Paris
1er Arrondissement
Phone: +33 / 1 / 55 35 33 90
www.colette.fr

Opening hours: Mon–Sat 11 am to 7 pm
Products: Exclusive fashion, perfumes, shoes, books; Water-bar
Public transportation: Métro 1 Tuileries
Map: No. 25

Russell James' Special Tip
Since 1997 Colette has led the style pack with eclectic, on-trend clothes, books, music and even water.

Colette reopened its doors in August 2008, freshly remodeled and enlarged. Spread over three floors, this temple of trends offers fashions and accessories, cosmetics, design and high tech, sneakers and street wear, magazines and gadgets, as well as art and books. Colette also regularly issues CD compilations and scented candles. It's a must!

Frisch renoviert und vergrößert hat das Colette im August 2008 wieder seine Pforten geöffnet. Auf drei Etagen bietet der Trendtempel Mode und Accessoires, Kosmetik, Design und High-Tech, Sneakers und Streetwear, Magazine und Gadgets sowie Kunst und Bücher. Zudem bringt Colette regelmäßig CD-Compilations und Duftkerzen heraus. Ein Muss!

Tout fraichement rénové et agrandi, colette a ouvert à nouveau ses portes en aout 2008. Ce temple de la mode offre sur trois étages mode et accessoires, cosmetique, design & high-tech, sneakers et streetwear, magazines et gadget, œuvres d'art et livres. Par ailleurs, Colette sort régulièrement ses compliations et de nouvelles bougies parfumées. Un must !

En agosto de 2008, la recién renovada y ampliada Colette abrió de nuevo sus puertas. En sus tres pisos, este templo de las tendencias ofrece moda y accesorios, cosmética, diseño, electrónica, zapatillas de deporte, ropa informal, revistas y gadgets, aparte de arte y libros. Además, Colette ofrece regularmente CD's recopilatorios y velas aromáticas. Una visita imprescindible.

Côté Bastide

4, rue de Poissy
75005 Paris
5e Arrondissement
Phone: +33 / 1 / 56 24 01 21
www.cotebastide.com

Opening hours: Mon–Sat 10:30 am to 7 pm, closed Mon+Wed 1 pm to 2 pm
Products: Provencal interior decoration, fabrics, tableware and everything for the bathroom
Public transportation: Métro 10 Cardinal Lemoine, Maubert Mutualité
Map: No. 26

Known in the past for his fragrant natural essences, today Côté Bastide also sells anything having to do with beautifying the home: candles, glasses, towels, linens, boxes, dishes, and much more. All products have a slightly nostalgic note in common. They are intended to awaken childhood memories so that customers will truly feel "at home" with Côté Bastide.

Früher bekannt für seine wohlriechenden Essenzen auf Naturbasis, vertreibt Côté Bastide heute zudem alles, was mit der Verschönerung des Wohnraums zu tun hat: Kerzen, Gläser, Tücher, Wäsche, Schachteln, Geschirr und vieles mehr. Allen Produkten ist eine leicht nostalgische Note gemein. So sollen Kindheitserinnerungen zum Leben erweckt werden, damit sich die Kunden mit Côté Bastide wirklich „zu Hause" fühlen.

Autrefois célèbre pour ses essences odorantes d'origine naturelle, Côté Bastide vend aujourd'hui, de surcroît, tout ce qui est en rapport avec l'embellissement des espaces intérieurs : bougies, verres, serviettes, linge, boîtes, vaisselle et beaucoup d'autres choses. Tous les produits ont en commun une note légèrement nostalgique. Ainsi, ce sont les souvenirs d'enfance qui veulent être ravivés pour qu'au Côté Bastide, le client se sente vraiment comme « à la maison ».

Conocido anteriormente por sus esencias aromáticas naturales, Côté Bastide comercia hoy con todo aquello que tenga algo que ver con el embellecimiento del hogar: velas, cristales, pañuelos, tejidos, cajas, cubiertos y mucho más. Todos los productos tienen en común una nota nostálgica, que busca evocar la infancia de los clientes para lograr que se sientan en Côté Bastide como "en casa".

Espace Kiliwatch

64, rue Tiquetonne
75002 Paris
2e Arrondissement
Phone: +33 / 1 / 42 21 17 37
www.espacekiliwatch.fr

Opening hours: Mon 2 pm to 7 pm, Tue–Sat 11 am to 7:30 pm
Products: Vintage clothes, bags, shoes, books, magazines and accessories
Public transportation: Métro 4 Etienne Marcel
Map: No. 27

Russell James' Special Tip
This painstakingly curated thrift shop mixes military surplus with vintage garments and punkish new pieces.

Espace Kiliwatch is another important address for vintage coolness. North of Les Halles, it offers old and made-to-look-old clothing for men and women, as well as bags, shoes, books, magazines, and accessories that are unparalleled and worth some serious rummaging. For just 30 euros you can find unusual shoes that you can be sure nobody else has. They now also have a store in Hamburg.

Auch das Espace Kiliwatch ist eine wichtige Anlaufstelle für Vintage-Coolness. Nördlich von Les Halles präsentiert es alte und auf alt gemachte Kleidung für Mann und Frau, dazu Taschen, Schuhe, Bücher, Magazine und Accessoires, die ihresgleichen suchen und zu intensivem Stöbern einladen. Schon für 30 Euro kann man hier ausgefallene Treter finden, die garantiert sonst niemand trägt. Mittlerweile gibt es auch eine Filiale in Hamburg.

L'Espace Kiliwatch, lui aussi, est un haut lieu du vintage cool. Situé au nord des Halles, il propose des vêtements deuxieme main ou vintage pour hommes et femmes, ainsi que sacs, chaussures, livres, magazines ou accessoires qui tous cherchent leur âme sœur et invitent à une fouille intensive. A partir de 30 euros, vous pouvez trouver ici des godillots qui vous auront tapé dans l'œil et que vous êtes sûrs de ne jamais voir portés ailleurs par quelqu'un d'autre. Il existe aussi, entre-temps, une filiale à Hambourg.

Espace Kiliwatch es también un importante punto para los amantes del vintage. Se encuentra al norte del mercado de Les Halles y ofrece ropa vieja y de estética desgastada tanto para hombre como para mujer, además de bolsos, zapatos, libros, magazines y accesorios exclusivos que incitan a rebuscar por todo el local. Por sólo 30 Euros se pueden encontrar aquí zapatos extravagantes, que seguro nadie más calza. También posee una filial en Hamburgo.

Galeries Lafayette

40, boulevard Haussmann
75009 Paris
9e Arrondissement
Phone: +33 / 1 / 42 82 34 56
www.galerieslafayette.com

Opening hours: Mon–Wed, Fri–Sat 9:30 am to 7:30 pm, Thu 9:30 am to 9 pm
Products: Department store
Public transportation: Métro 7, 9 Chausée d'Antin – La Fayette
Map: No. 28

Since opening at the end of the 19th century, Galeries Lafayette has offered a sophisticated, constantly changing assortment of famous but affordable brands covering all areas: fashion, home décor, and beauty and gourmet products. The department store is the largest in the Western world. With its 110-feet-high neo-Byzantine glass cupola, it is the second-most-frequently visited attraction after the Louvre in Paris.

Seit ihrer Eröffnung Ende des 19. Jahrhunderts bieten die Galeries Lafayette ein differenziertes, ständig wechselndes Sortiment an renommierten, aber auch erschwinglichen Marken, das sämtliche Bereiche umfasst: Mode, Schönes fürs Heim, Beauty- und Gourmet-Produkte. Das Kaufhaus ist das größte der westlichen Welt. Mit seiner 33 Meter hohen Glaskuppel im neobyzantinischen Stil ist es nach dem Louvre die am häufigsten besuchte Sehenswürdigkeit von Paris.

Depuis leur création à la fin du XIXème siècle, les Galeries Lafayette offrent une sélection subtile et sans cesse renouvelée de marques, des plus prestigieuses aux plus accessibles dans tous les secteurs : femme, homme, enfant, beauté, maison et gourmet. Le grand magasin est le plus grand du monde occidental et abrite une coupole néo-byzantine de 33 mètres de haut. Il est le second site le plus visité à Paris après le Louvre.

Desde su inauguración a finales del siglo XIX, las Galeries Lafayette ofrecen un surtido diferenciado y en permanente renovación, tanto de marcas de renombre como de otras más asequibles, que abarca todos los campos: moda, bonitos artículos para el hogar, artículos de belleza y productos para gourmets. Estos grandes almacenes son los mayores del mundo occidental. Con su cúpula de cristal de estilo neobizantino de 33 metros de altura, los almacenes son el monumento más visitado después del Museo del Louvre.

John Galliano

384/386, rue Saint-Honoré
75001 Paris
1er Arrondissement
Phone: +33 / 1 / 55 35 40 40
www.johngalliano.com

Opening hours: Mon–Sat 11 am to 7 pm
Products: High-range prêt-à-porter
Public transportation: Métro 1, 8, 12 Concorde
Map: No. 29

Since 2003, British fashion designer John Galliano's first boutique of his own has joined the ranks of the exclusive stores on Rue Saint-Honoré in Paris, and yet stands out from them. Conceived by architect Jean-Michel Wilmotte, the shop surprises with its simplicity and fascinates with amusing details. Fashion-wise, Galliano remains true to himself under his own name, as well; it has to be unusual.

Seit 2003 reiht sich die erste eigene Boutique des britischen Modedesigners John Galliano in die Reihe der exklusiven Geschäfte der Rue Saint-Honoré in Paris ein, und sticht doch aus ihnen hervor. Konzipiert von Architekt Jean-Michel Wilmotte überrascht das Geschäft durch seine Schlichtheit und fasziniert durch amüsante Details. Modisch bleibt sich Galliano auch unter eigenem Namen treu: ausgefallen muss es sein.

En 2003, le designer de mode britannique John Galliano ouvrit sa première boutique qui prit alors place parmi les magasins selects de la rue Saint-Honoré à Paris tout en s'en distinguant fortement. Conçue par l'architecte Jean-Michel Wilmotte, la boutique surprend par sa sobriété et fascine par ses détails amusants. Quand à ses collections de mode, Galliano reste fidèle à lui-même et à son nom : il faut que cela se fasse remarquer.

Desde 2003, la boutique del diseñador de moda británico John Galliano destaca entre las tiendas más exclusivas de la Rue Saint-Honoré en París. Concebida por el arquitecto Jean-Michel Wilmotte, la tienda sorprende por su sencillez y fascina a través de divertidos detalles. Galliano se mantiene fiel a sí mismo, dando a la tienda el toque de extravagancia que le caracteriza.

Ladurée (Saint-Germain)

21, rue Bonaparte
75006 Paris
6e Arrondissement
Phone: +33 / 1 / 44 07 64 87
www.laduree.com

Opening hours: Mon–Fri 8:30 am to 7:30 pm, Sat 8:30 am to 8:30 pm, Sun and public holidays 10 am to 7:30 pm; Chocolaterie daily 10 am to 7 pm
Products: French traditional pâtisserie, macarons, chocolates
Public transportation: Métro 4 Saint-Germain-des-Prés
Map: No. 30

Lovers of cultivated tea culture should stop at one of the Ladurée Salons. Richly decorated, the decor is reminiscent of bygone times; after all, the first Ladurée bakery opened in 1862. A filled round cookie called "macaron" has become a symbol of the establishment, delighting eyes and palates in a variety of colors and flavors.

Liebhaber des gepflegten Teetrinkens sollten einen Stopp in einem der Ladurée-Salons machen. Reich verziert, erinnert die Einrichtung an vergangene Zeiten – schließlich wurde die erste Bäckerei Ladurée bereits 1862 eröffnet. Zu einem Symbol des Hauses ist ein gefüllter runder Keks mit Namen „Macaron" geworden, der in verschiedenen Farben und Geschmacksrichtungen Augen und Gaumen verzückt.

Les amoureux du thé et du cérémonial s'en dégageant devraient faire une halte dans l'un des salons Ladurée. Richement décoré, l'aménagement rappelle les temps anciens – en effet, la première pâtisserie Ladurée ouvrait déjà ses portes en 1862. Le petit biscuit rond fourré, de plusieurs couleurs et aux goûts différents, appelé « macaron » est devenu le symbole de la maison et constitue un plaisir autant pour le palais que pour les yeux.

Aquellos que sepan disfrutar de una buena taza de té en un ambiente refinado deben hacer un alto en uno de los salones Ladurée. El mobiliario, ricamente decorado, evoca tiempos pasados –después de todo, la primera panadería Ladurée abrió sus puertas en 1862. El símbolo de la casa es una galleta rellena con forma redonda llamada "Macaron", disponible en diferentes colores y sabores que cautivan tanto los ojos como el paladar.

Louis Vuitton

101, avenue des Champs-Elysées
75008 Paris
8e Arrondissement
Phone: +33 / 8 / 10 81 00 10
www.louisvuitton.com

Opening hours: Mon–Sat 10 am to 8 pm, Sun 11 am to 7 pm
Products: Clothes, shoes and accessories
Public transportation: Métro 1 George V
Map: No. 31

We used to associate Louis Vuitton primarily with exclusive luggage. While the bags with the famous LV logo are still the firm's trademark, the label also produces elegant fashions, shoes and accessories such as sunglasses and jewelry. The boutique on the Champs-Elysées gives an impression of the brand's luxury: if you have the right wallet it leaves no desire unfulfilled.

Früher verband man mit Louis Vuitton vor allem exklusives Reisegepäck. Zwar sind die Taschen mit dem berühmten LV-Print auch heute noch das Markenzeichen des Hauses, doch stellt das Label zudem elegante Mode, Schuhe sowie Accessoires wie Sonnenbrillen oder Schmuck her. Einen Eindruck vom Luxus der Marke vermittelt die Boutique auf den Champs-Elysées, die bei entsprechendem Geldbeutel keine Wünsche offen lässt.

Autrefois, on associait avec Louis Vuitton surtout les sacs de voyage luxueux. Certes, les sacs portant le célèbre monogramme LV sont encore le signe distinctif de la maison, mais le label produit aussi des vêtements de mode élégants, des chaussures et des accessoires tels que des lunettes ou des bijoux. La boutique sur les Champs-Elysées communique l'image de luxe de la marque, laquelle, en fonction de votre porte-monnaie, exauce tous vos désirs.

Hasta hace poco, Louis Vuitton era sinónimo de equipajes exclusivos. Los bolsos con el famoso logotipo LV siguen siendo hoy en día el emblema de la casa, pero la firma crea también moda elegante, calzado y complementos como gafas de sol y joyas. Una muestra del lujo que rodea a la marca es su boutique en los Campos Elíseos, en la que ningún deseo se queda por satisfacer, siempre y cuando el monedero lo permita.

Printemps

64, boulevard Haussmann
75009 Paris
9e Arrondissement
Phone: +33 / 1 / 42 82 50 00
www.printemps.fr

Opening hours: Mon–Sat 9.35 am to 8 pm, Thu 9.35 am to 10 pm
Products: Department store
Public transportation: Métro 9 Havre Caumartin
Map: No. 32

Directly behind the opera is Printemps: a department store from the 19th century that already captivates us with its facade and painted glass cupolas. And the range of merchandise leaves hardly any wish unfulfilled. In addition, Printemps offers discount weeks several times a year, when most products—not just clothing—are generously reduced. It's definitely worth dropping by.

Direkt hinter der Oper liegt das Printemps – ein Kaufhaus aus dem vorletzten Jahrhundert, das schon durch seine Fassade und seine bemalte gläserne Kuppel besticht. Doch auch das Warenangebot lässt kaum Wünsche offen. Außerdem bietet das Printemps mehrmals im Jahr Rabattwochen an, bei denen die meisten Produkte, und eben nicht nur Kleidung, großzügig reduziert werden. Vorbeischauen lohnt sich deshalb in jedem Fall.

Juste derrière l'opéra se trouve le Printemps, grand magasin datant de l'avant-dernier siècle, qui déjà, séduit à la seule vue de sa façade et de sa coupole peinte en verre. Quand à l'éventail de choix des produits, il ne laissera aucun de vos désirs inassouvi. Par ailleurs, plusieurs fois par an, le Printemps a ses semaines de soldes, pendant lesquelles les prix de la plupart des produits, et pas seulement dans le domaine du prêt-à-porter, sont généreusement réduits. Cela vaut la peine, en tous les cas, d'y jeter un coup d'œil.

Justo detrás de la Ópera se encuentra el Printemps, un gran almacén del siglo XIX, que con su fachada y su cúpula de cristales multicolor impresiona ya desde fuera. Pero el surtido de productos que se ofrece en el interior no es menos espectacular. Además, el Printemps está de rebajas varias semanas al año, durante las cuales la mayoría de los productos, y no sólo la ropa, ofrecen generosos descuentos. Merece la pena darse una vuelta por allí.

Salons du Palais Royal Shiseido

Jardins du Palais Royal
142, galerie Valois – 25, rue de Valois
75001 Paris
1er Arrondissement
Phone: +33 / 1 / 49 27 09 09
www.salons-shiseido.com

Opening hours: Mon–Sat 10 am to 7 pm
Products: Perfumes Serge Lutens
Public transportation: M° 1, 7 Palais Royal Musée du Louvre
Map: No. 33

Shiseido opened this exclusive fragrance salon in the historic Palais Royal in the middle of Paris in the early 90s. The interior was designed down to the most minute detail by fragrance creator Serge Lutens. It's also he who is responsible each year for the emergence of two new fragrances, one of which is created exclusively for the Palais Royal. Insiders place their orders through the website.

Anfang der neunziger Jahre eröffnete Shiseido im historischen Palais Royal mitten in Paris diesen exklusiven Duftsalon. Das Innere wurde bis ins kleinste Detail von Duftkreateur Serge Lutens gestaltet. Er ist es auch, der jedes Jahr für die Entstehung von zwei neuen Düften verantwortlich ist, von denen einer exklusiv für das Palais Royal kreiert wird. Insider bestellen über die Internetseite.

Au début des années quatre-vingt-dix, Shiseido ouvrit cette parfumerie raffinée dans l'historique Palais Royal, situé en plein cœur de Paris. L'intérieur a été conçu, jusque dans ses moindres détails, par le créateur de parfums Serge Lutens. C'est lui qui, chaque année, est à l'origine de deux nouveaux parfums, dont l'un est créé exclusivement pour le Palais Royal. Les initiés passent leurs commandes sur la page Internet.

A comienzos de los 90, Shiseido abrió esta exclusiva perfumería en el histórico Palais Royal en pleno centro de París. El interior fue planeado hasta el último detalle por el creador de aromas Serge Lutens, responsable a su vez de crear cada año dos nuevos perfumes, uno de los cuales está pensado en exclusiva para el Palais Royal. Los entendidos realizan sus pedidos por internet.

Viaduc des Arts

1–129, avenue Daumesnil
75012 Paris
12e Arrondissement
Phone: +33 / 1 / 44 75 80 66
www.viaduc-des-arts.fr

Opening hours: Mon–Sat 10 am to 7 pm
Products: Arts and crafts are exhibited and sold in 51 studios
Public transportation: Métro 1, 5 Bastille; RER A, D Gare de Lyon
Map: No. 34

About fifty artists and craftsmen took over the former viaduct of the railway line between the Bastille and Vincennes, using the renovated and glassed-in arches as studios or exhibition spaces for their works of wood, glass, leather, copper, iron, or fabric. There are regular exhibits and events, and the landscaped promenade above the boutique roofs makes for a nice stroll.

Rund 50 Künstler und Handwerker haben sich den ehemaligen Viadukt der Eisenbahnlinie zwischen Bastille und Vincennes zu eigen gemacht und nutzen die renovierten und verglasten Bögen als Atelier oder Ausstellungsraum für ihre Werke aus Holz, Glas, Leder, Kupfer, Eisen oder Stoff. Regelmäßig finden Ausstellungen und Veranstaltungen statt, und über den Dächern der Boutiquen lädt die begrünte Promenade zu einem Bummel ein.

Une cinquantaine d'artistes et d'artisans se sont approprié l'ancien viaduc de la voie de chemin de fer situé entre la Bastille et Vincennes pour faire des arches rénovées et vitrées leurs ateliers ou salles d'exposition de leurs œuvres, que celles-ci soient en bois, verre, cuir, cuivre, fer ou en tissu. Des expositions et des événements y ont régulièrement lieu et, sur le toit, au-dessus des boutiques, une promenade verdoyante invite à la flânerie.

Alrededor de 50 artistas y artesanos han tomado el antiguo viaducto de la línea del tranvía entre la Bastilla y la ciudad de Vincennes utilizando los renovados arcos acristalados como atelier o sala de exposiciones para sus obras en madera, cristal, cuero, cobre, hierro o tela. Se celebran con regularidad exposiciones y eventos, y el paseo ajardinado sobre los tejados de las boutiques invita a dar una vuelta.

Wochdom

72, rue Condorcet
75009 Paris
9e Arrondissement
Phone: +33 / 1 / 53 21 01 19
www.wochdom.com

Opening hours: Mon–Sat noon to 8 pm
Products: Vintage fashion, shoes, accessories and books
Public transportation: Métro 2, 12 Pigalle
Map: No. 35

Clothing, shoes, bags, magazines, posters, and books, that's the range of merchandise sold at Wochdom in its two-part shop. This vintage temple is pleasantly distinguished from similar shops by its sleek black décor and well arranged presentation of the various articles.

Kleidung, Schuhe, Taschen, Zeitschriften, Poster und Bücher – das ist das Angebot, das Wochdom in seinem zweigeteilten Geschäft verkauft. Dabei hebt sich der Vintage-Tempel durch sein schlichtes schwarzes Dekor und die übersichtliche Präsentation der verschiedenen Artikel angenehm von ähnlich sortierten Geschäften ab.

Vêtements, chaussures, sacs, magazines, posters et livres : c'est ce que vous propose Wochdom dans son magasin réparti sur deux pieces. Ce temple du vintage se distingue d'autres magasins similaires par son décor simple, noir, et par l'agréable et claire présentation des différents articles.

Ropa, zapatos, bolsos, revistas, carteles y libros, esa es la oferta de Wochdom en su tienda, dividida en dos secciones. Este templo del vintage se diferencia agradablemente de otras tiendas similares por su sencilla decoración en color negro y por la ordenada presentación de los diferentes artículos.

HIGHLIGHTS

Cimetière du Père Lachaise

16, rue du Repos
75020 Paris
20e Arrondissement
Phone: +33 / 1 / 55 25 82 10
www.pere-lachaise.com

Opening hours: 16th March to 5th November Mon–Fri 8 am to 5:30 pm, Sat 8:30 am to 5:30 pm; 6th November to 15th March Mon–Fri 8 am to 6 pm, Sat 8:30 am to 6 pm, Sun and public holidays 9 am to 6 pm
Public transportation: Métro 2, 3 Père-Lachaise   **Map:** No. 36

Russell James' Special Tip
More than 300,000 people are buried in Paris' biggest cemetery, notably Oscar Wilde and Jim Morrison.

Since 1804, many famous people have found their final—and sometimes very artistically designed—resting place in this cemetery, the largest in Paris. The interment roster includes La Fontaine, Chopin, Balzac and Edith Piaf. You receive a map at the entrance showing the roughly 200 famous people buried here, and can then take a nostalgic walk along the lovely winding paths.

Viele Berühmtheiten haben seit 1804 auf diesem größten Pariser Friedhof ihre letzte, mitunter überaus kunstvoll gestaltete Ruhestätte gefunden – darunter La Fontaine, Chopin, Balzac und Edith Piaf. Am Eingang erhält man einen Plan mit den rund 200 hier begrabenen Berühmtheiten und kann sich dann auf einen nostalgischen Spaziergang durch die schönen, gewundenen Alleen begeben.

Depuis 1804, beaucoup de célébrités ont trouvé ici, dans ce cimetière qui est le plus grand de Paris, leur dernière demeure – entre autres La Fontaine, Chopin, Balzac et Edith Piaf. Certains de ces tombeaux sont extrêmement décorés et avec beaucoup d'art. Une fois qu'on vous aura donné, à l'entrée, le plan indiquant les quelques 200 célébrités enterrées ici, vous pourrez vous laisser aller à une promenade nostalgique à travers les belles allées sinueuses.

Desde 1804, multitud de famosos han encontrado en el mayor de los cementerios parisinos su última y en ocasiones sumamente bella morada, entre ellos La Fontaine, Chopin, Balzac y Edith Piaf. En la entrada se recibe un plano con las alrededor de 200 personalidades aquí enterradas, siendo posible realizar a continuación un nostálgico paseo por los preciosos y sinuosos paseos.

Centre Georges Pompidou

19, rue Beaubourg
75004 Paris
4e Arrondissement
Phone: +33 / 1 / 44 78 12 33
www.centrepompidou.com / www.parismuseumpass.fr

Opening hours: Wed–Mon 11 am to 10 pm, closed on 1st May
Public transportation: Métro 11 Rambuteau
Map: No. 37

Conceived by Renzo Piano and Richard Rogers and controversial in the 70s for its futuristic construction, Centre Pompidou is now a firmly established fixture in Paris. Behind brightly colored tubes, metal rods and glass, the museum of modern art houses numerous works by famous artists of the 20th century. From the top you can enjoy the view of Paris and jugglers display their skills in the forecourt.

In den siebziger Jahren wegen seiner futuristischen Bauweise umstritten, ist das von Renzo Piano und Richard Rogers konzipierte Centre Pompidou heute aus Paris nicht wegzudenken. Hinter bunten Röhren, Metallgestänge und Glas beherbergt das Museum für Moderne Kunst zahlreiche Werke berühmter Künstler des 20. Jahrhunderts; von oben genießt man den Blick auf Paris und auf dem Vorplatz zeigen Jongleure ihr Können.

Alors qu'il était contesté dans les années soixante-dix en raison de sa construction futuriste, on ne peut aujourd'hui imaginer Paris sans le centre Pompidou, conçu par Renzo Piano et Richard Rogers. Derrière ses tubes, ses armatures et ses verres colorés, le musée d'art moderne abrite de nombreuses œuvres d'artistes célèbres du 20ème siècle. D'en haut, on peut jouir d'une vue sur Paris ; sur l'esplanade, des jongleurs exhibent leur savoir-faire.

Polémico en los setenta por su estilo futurista, el Centro Pompidou, concebido por Renzo Piano y Richard Rogers, es hoy en día un símbolo de París. El museo de arte moderno oculta tras tubos de colores, armazones de metal y cristal numerosas obras de famosos artistas del siglo XX. Desde la parte superior se puede disfrutar de un fantástico panorama sobre París mientras los malabaristas muestran sus habilidades en la explanada frente al edificio.

Centre
Pompidou

LE
MOUVEMENT
DES
IMAGES

ART. CINÉMA
5 avril 2006 – 29 janvier 2007

CANAL+

Champ de Mars

Tour Eiffel
75007 Paris
7e Arrondissement
www.paris.fr

Public transportation: Métro 6 Champ de Mars — Tour Eiffel / Bir-Hakeim
Map: No. 38

There are few places where you can relax in such a spectacular setting as on the Field of Mars, the eye glides almost automatically to the Eiffel Tower and Trocadéro. This used to be a place for military parades, but nowadays there are regular concerts by international musicians. During large celebrations such as the French national holiday on July 14th, up to 800,000 people crowd into the expansive space.

An wenigen Orten kann man vor so traumhafter Kulisse entspannen wie auf dem Marsfeld – fast automatisch gleitet der Blick zu Eiffelturm und Trocadéro. Wo früher Militärparaden abgehalten wurden, finden heute regelmäßig Konzerte internationaler Musiker statt. Bei großen Feiern, wie zum französischen Nationalfeiertag am 14. Juli, drängen sich dann schon mal bis zu 800.000 Menschen auf der weitläufigen Anlage.

Il existe peu d'endroits qui, comme le Champ de Mars, vous permettent de vous ressourcer devant des coulisses prêtant tant au rêve – de là, le regard glisse automatiquement sur la Tour Eiffel et le Trocadéro. Alors qu'autrefois avaient lieu ici les parades militaires, aujourd'hui, des concerts de musiciens à la renommée mondiale y sont régulièrement donnés. Lors de grandes occasions, comme la fête nationale du 14 juillet, près de 800 000 personnes affluent sur ce champ si spacieux.

En pocos lugares es posible relajarse teniendo de fondo una escena tan espectacular como en el parque del Campo de Marte. La mirada se desvía casi automáticamente hacia la Torre Eiffel y la Plaza del Trocadéro. El lugar, que antiguamente estuvo destinado a los desfiles militares, sirve a menudo hoy en día de escenario para conciertos de músicos internacionales. Con motivo de celebraciones especiales, como la Fiesta de la Federación del 14 de julio, se llegan a juntar hasta 800.000 personas en las extensas instalaciones del parque.

Jardin du Luxembourg

Rue de Médicis, rue de Vaugirard
75006 Paris
6e Arrondissement
www.paris.fr

Opening hours: Daily 7:30 am to 9:45 pm (summer), 8:15 am to 4:45 pm (winter)
Public transportation: Métro 12 Notre-Dame-des-Champs
Map: No. 39

Russell James' Special Tip
The garden is a refuge for young and old, with blooming flowers, a merry-go-round and spouting fountains.

With its geometric lawns and lush flower beds, the Jardin du Luxembourg, or Luxembourg Gardens, is a typical French garden. Especially popular are the spaces around the large fountain where children sail toy boats. For locals and tourists alike, the gardens are the perfect place to relax, take in the many sculptures, and enjoy a bit of the Parisian way of life.

Mit seinen geometrischen Rasenflächen und den üppigen Blumenbeeten ist der Jardin du Luxembourg ein typisch französischer Garten. Besonders beliebt sind die Plätze um das große Bassin, in dem Kinder kleine Modellboote segeln lassen. Für Einheimische und Touristen ist der Jardin ein idealer Ort, um sich auszuruhen, die zahlreichen Skulpturen zu betrachten und ein wenig die Pariser Lebensart zu genießen.

Avec ses gazons géométriques et ses parterres de fleurs luxuriants, le jardin du Luxembourg est un jardin typiquement français. Ce sont surtout les environs du grand bassin, là où les enfants font naviguer leurs bateaux, qui sont particulièrement prisés. Aussi bien pour les Parisiens que pour les touristes, c'est l'endroit idéal pour se reposer en contemplant les nombreuses sculptures et pour profiter un peu de l'art de vivre parisien.

Con sus praderas de césped geométricas y sus exuberantes planteles de flores, el Jardin de Luxembourg es el típico jardín francés. Especialmente apreciadas son las zonas junto al gran estanque, donde los niños se divierten con sus pequeños barcos de juguete. Tanto para los nativos como para los turistas, el jardín es el lugar ideal donde poder relajarse, contemplar las numerosas esculturas y disfrutar un poco del estilo de vida parisino.

La Villette, Cité des Sciences

30, avenue Corentin-Cariou
75019 Paris
19e Arrondissement
Phone: +33 / 1 / 40 03 75 75
www.cite-sciences.com / www.parismuseumpass.fr

Opening hours: Tue–Sat 10 am to 6 pm, Sun 10 am to 7 pm
Public transportation: Métro 7 Porte de la Villette
Map: No. 40

In place of the former slaughterhouse, this futuristic amusement park rises in the northeast part of the city and includes, among other things, the largest science and technology museum of its kind. Scientific phenomena are made easily understandable here, and you can try out many things yourself. Fascinating features of the park include the enormous spherical movie theater and cubic structures that serve as a children's atelier or café.

Anstelle des ehemaligen Schlachthofs erhebt sich im Nordosten der Stadt dieser futuristische Freizeitpark, unter anderem mit dem größten Wissenschafts- und Technikmuseum seiner Art. Naturwissenschaftliche Phänomene werden hier leicht verständlich erklärt, zudem kann vieles selbst ausprobiert werden. Im Park faszinieren das kugelförmige Riesenkino sowie rote Würfelbauten, die als Kinderateliers oder Café dienen.

C'est à la place de l'ancien abattoir que se dresse aujourd'hui, au nord-est de la ville, ce parc de loisirs futuriste abritant, entre autre, le plus grand musée, dans son genre, de sciences et de technique. Des phénomènes de sciences naturelles sont ici expliqués de façon pédagogique et beaucoup d'entre eux peuvent être expérimentés par les visiteurs eux-mêmes. Particulièrement fascinants sont la géode, cet énorme cinéma en forme de boule, et les constructions rouges en forme de dés, à l'intérieur desquels on trouve, soit des garderies, soit des cafés.

Este futurista parque de atracciones se levanta en el noreste de la ciudad, allí donde antiguamente se encontraba el matadero, albergando entre otras cosas el mayor museo científico-técnico de su clase. Los fenómenos científicos son explicados aquí de forma muy sencilla, y además es posible experimentar con muchas cosas personalmente. En el parque fascinan el enorme cine esférico y los edificios *Folies* con forma de cubos de color rojo, que sirven de guarderías o cafés.

Espace

Marches du Sacré-Cœur

Parvis du Sacré-Cœur
35, rue du Chevalier-de-la-Barre
75018 Paris
18e Arrondissement
www.paris.fr

Public transportation: Métro 2 Anvers, 12 Abesses
Map: No. 41

The symbol of Montmartre is the Sacré-Cœur basilica, but the steps below the church have developed an equal attraction of their own for tourists and locals alike. Sun-worshipers and souvenir vendors cavort on the expansive stairs with its panoramic view of Paris. Clowns and musicians provide entertainment.

Das Wahrzeichen des Montmartre-Hügels ist die Kirche Sacré-Cœur, doch die Treppen unterhalb des Gotteshauses sind mittlerweile zu einem gleichwertigen Anziehungspunkt geworden – und zwar für Touristen und Einheimische gleichermaßen. Mit Blick auf ganz Paris tummeln sich auf der weitläufigen Treppe Sonnenanbeter und Souvenirverkäufer. Für gute Unterhaltung sorgen Clowns und Musiker.

L'emblème de la butte Montmartre, c'est bien la basilique du Sacré-Cœur. Cependant, les escaliers situés en amont de la maison de Dieu sont devenus entre-temps un point d'attraction tout aussi intéressant, et ce, autant pour les touristes que pour les Parisiens. Ces escaliers offrent une vue sur tout Paris et grouillent d'adeptes du bronzage et de marchands de souvenirs. Pour ce qui est de l'ambiance, des clowns et des musiciens s'en chargent.

El monumento característico de la colina Montmartre es la iglesia Sacré-Cœur. Sin embargo, las escaleras bajo el templo se han convertido en un lugar igualmente atractivo, tanto para los turistas como para los habitantes de la ciudad. Sobre los peldaños de la larga escalera, desde la cual se puede divisar todo París, se amontonan los amantes del sol y los vendedores de souvenirs. Payasos y músicos entretienen al público con su arte.

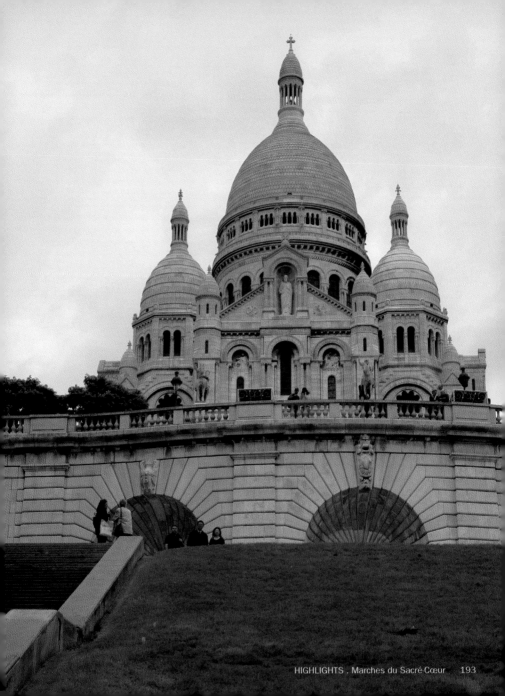

Musée Rodin

Hôtel Biron
79, rue de Varenne
75007 Paris
7e Arrondissement
Phone: +33 / 1 / 44 18 61 10
www.musee-rodin.com / www.parismuseumpass.fr

Opening hours: April to Sept Tue–Sun 9:30 am to 5:45 pm; Oct to March Tue–Sun 9:30 am to 4:45 pm
Public transportation: Métro 6 Varenne
Map: No. 42

Sculptor Auguste Rodin lived in this grand rococo palace together with other artists from 1908 until his death in 1917. In addition to his works, the museum also shows those of his pupil and longtime lover Camille Claudel. Additional sculptures, including Rodin's famous "Thinker," are installed in the attractively designed gardens. The café invites you to relax beneath shady trees.

In dem prachtvollen Rokoko-Palais lebte der Bildhauer Auguste Rodin zusammen mit anderen Künstlern von 1908 bis zu seinem Tod 1917. Neben seinen Werken zeigt das Museum auch die seiner Schülerin und langjährigen Geliebten Camille Claudel. Weitere Skulpturen, darunter Rodins berühmter „Denker", finden sich im hübsch angelegten Garten. Unter Schatten spendenden Bäumen lädt die Cafeteria zum Verweilen ein.

C'est dans le somptueux palais rococo qu'a vécu le sculpteur Auguste Rodin avec d'autres artistes de 1908 jusqu'en 1917, année de sa mort. Le musée présente, à coté de ses œuvres, aussi celles de Camille Claudel qui fut son élève et, pendant plusieurs années, son amante. D'autres sculptures, entre autres le célèbre « Penseur » de Rodin, ont été placées dans le jardin joliment aménagé. À l'ombre d'arbres généreux, la cafétéria invite à s'attarder autour d'un verre.

El escultor Auguste Rodin vivió, desde 1908 hasta su muerte en 1917, en este lujoso palacio acompañado de otros artistas. Junto a sus obras se exponen también las de su alumna, y durante muchos años amante, Camille Claudel. En el precioso jardín se encuentran otras esculturas, entre ellas el famoso "Pensador" del propio Rodin. Las sombras de los árboles invitan a quedarse un rato en la cafetería.

LE PENSEVR
DE RODIN OFFERT
PAR SOVSCRIPTION
PVBLIQVE AV PEVPLE
DE PARIS MCMVI

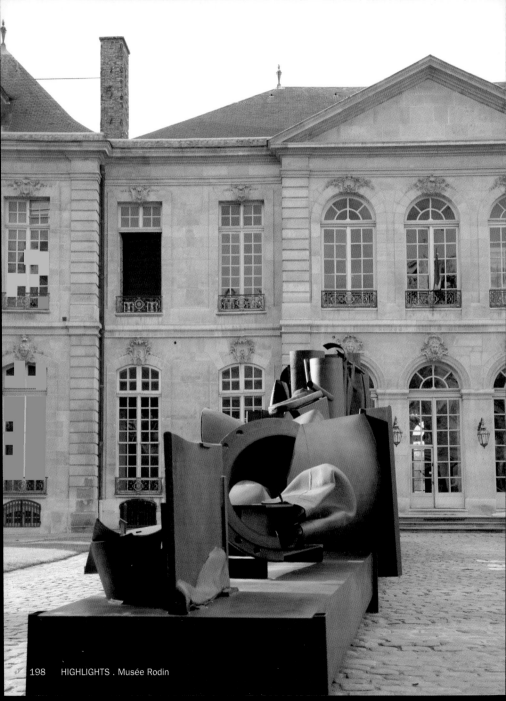

Palais de Tokyo

13, avenue du Président Wilson
75116 Paris
16e Arrondissement
Phone: +33 / 1 / 47 23 38 86
www.palaisdetokyo.com

Opening hours: Tue–Sun noon to midnight, closed 1st January, 1st May and 25th December
Public transportation: Métro 9 Iéna
Map: No. 43

With its cracked concrete floors and visible utility pipes, the Palais de Tokyo exudes a certain construction-site charm that does not detract from the building in any way. It has become a favored venue for the young art scene, with impressive painting, photography, video, fashion, literature, and dance exhibits. Adapting to its audience, the Palais is open until midnight.

Mit rissigen Betonböden und sichtbaren Versorgungsrohren versprüht das Palais de Tokyo einen gewissen Baustellencharme, der dem Haus alles andere als abträglich ist: Es ist mittlerweile zum Lieblingstreffpunkt der jungen Kunstszene geworden und beeindruckt mit seinen Ausstellungen zu Malerei, Fotografie, Video, Mode, Literatur oder Tanz. Zugeschnitten auf sein Publikum, hat das Palais bis Mitternacht geöffnet.

Avec son sol en béton fissuré et son réseau visible de tuyaux, le Palais de Tokyo dégage un certain charme rappelant l'ambiance des chantiers, ce qui est loin de nuire à l'intérêt de l'édifice : il est d'ailleurs devenu le point de rencontre favori des jeunes artistes et propose d'impressionnantes expositions dans des domaines tels que la peinture, la photographie, la vidéo, la mode, la littérature ou la danse. À l'image de son public couche-tard, le palais est ouvert jusqu'à minuit.

Con sus suelos de hormigón agrietados y sus tubos de abastecimiento a plena vista, el centro de arte Palais de Tokyo tiene un cierto encanto de edificio en construcción, que sin embargo no le ha perjudicado en absoluto, pues se ha convertido en el punto de encuentro favorito de la joven escena artística e impresiona con sus exposiciones de pintura, fotografía, video, moda, literatura o danza. El Palais está hecho a la medida de su público y sus puertas permanecen abiertas hasta la media noche.

PALAIS
DE
TOKYO

Puces de Saint-Ouen-Clignancourt

Porte de Clignancourt, rue des Entrepots
75018 Paris
18e Arrondissement
www.paris.fr

Opening hours: Sat–Mon 7 am to 7 pm
Public transportation: Métro 4 Porte de Clignancourt
Map: No. 44

The largest and most famous flea market in Paris is the Puces de Saint-Ouen. On weekends thousands of visitors crowd through the labyrinth of halls, lanes, and shops in search of rummage, secondhand clothes, books, or art deco objects. Even though the flea market is controlled by professional dealers nowadays, there is still a rousing carnival atmosphere.

Der berühmteste und größte Flohmarkt in Paris ist der Puces de Saint-Ouen. Tausende von Besuchern drängen sich am Wochenende durch das Labyrinth aus Hallen, Gassen und Geschäften, auf der Suche nach Trödel, Secondhandklamotten, Büchern oder Art-déco-Gegenständen. Auch wenn der Flohmarkt heute von professionellen Händlern bestimmt wird, herrscht noch immer eine mitreißende Jahrmarkt-atmosphäre.

Ce sont les puces les plus importantes et les plus connues de Paris. Le weekend, des milliers de visiteurs se bousculent à travers le labyrinthe de halls, ruelles et boutiques, à la recherche de bric-à-brac, de vêtements d'occasion, de livres ou d'objets Art déco. Même si les puces sont aujourd'hui aux mains de marchands professionnels, il y règne encore une ambiance fascinante de foire.

El Puces de Saint-Ouen es el mercadillo más famoso y extenso de París. Los fines de semana se concentran en el laberinto de pabellones, callejuelas y tiendas miles de visitantes en busca de gangas, ropa de segunda mano, libros o artículos de estilo art déco. Aunque hoy en día el mercadillo está dominado por vendedores profesionales, sigue predominando una vibrante atmósfera de feria anual.

Place des Vosges

Place des Vosges
75003 Paris
3e Arrondissement
www.paris.fr

Public transportation: Métro 1 Saint-Paul or Bastille
Map: No. 45

Among the most charming locations in Paris is the Place des Vosges. Red, three-story brick buildings adorn the four sides; at ground level, you can rummage in shops beneath attractive arcades. There's no shortage of culture, either: today the Victor Hugo Museum is located at No. 6, where the author lived for many years. After the museum visit one can relax in the park.

Zu den charmantesten Plätzen in Paris gehört die Place des Vosges. Dreistöckige rote Backsteinhäuser zieren die vier Seiten, im Erdgeschoss kann man unter hübschen Arkaden in Geschäften stöbern. Doch auch die Kultur kommt nicht zu kurz : im Haus Nummer 6, in dem der Schriftsteller viele Jahre lang lebte, befindet sich heute das Victor-Hugo-Museum. Nach dem Museumsbesuch kann man es sich im Park gemütlich machen.

La Place des Vosges fait partie des places les plus charmantes de Paris. Des maisons en briques rouges à trois étages tapissent les quatre cotés : au rez-de-chaussée, sous les arcades, vous pouvez flâner dans les magasins. Même à un niveau culturel, vous serez comblé : au numéro 6, dans la maison où a vécu l'écrivain pendant plusieurs années, se trouve aujourd'hui le musée Victor Hugo. Après sa visite, vous pourrez aller vous détendre dans le parc.

La Place des Vosges, flanqueada por edificios de tres alturas construidos con ladrillo rojo, es uno de los lugares más encantadores de París. Las preciosas arcadas de la planta baja están llenas de tiendas, pero también hay espacio para la cultura; en la casa número 6, durante años residencia del escritor Victor Hugo, se encuentra el museo que lleva su nombre. Tras visitar el museo, nada mejor que ponerse cómodo en el parque.

ARRIVAL IN PARIS

By Plane

There are two international airports in the city area.
Information:
Phone: +33 / 39 50 www.aeroportsdeparis.fr

Paris Charles de Gaulle (CDG)
Situated 25 km (5.5 miles) north of downtown Paris.
With RER trains line B from Terminal 1 and 2, departing every 10–15 mins, via Gare du Nord to Châtelet-
Les Halles station in the city center, traveling time
approx. 30 mins. With Roissybus from Terminal 1, 2
and 3, departing every 15–20 mins to Opéra station,
traveling time approx. 45–60 mins. With Air France
coaches e.g. every 12 mins to Arc de Triomphe,
traveling time 40 mins (www.carsairfrance.com). A
cab ride to downtown Paris costs approx. € 50 (extra
charge of approx. 15 % from 7 pm to 7 am and on
weekends).

Paris Orly (ORY)
Situated approx. 16 km (10 miles) south of the city
center. With RER line Orlyval departing every 4–7
mins to Antony station, then changing to RER line B
to Châtelet-Les Halles station in the center, traveling
time approx. 35 mins. With shuttle buses departing
every 15 mins to RER station Pont de Rungis, then
change to RER line C to Gare d'Austerlitz, traveling
time approx. 35 mins. With Orlybus departing every
15–20 mins to RER station Denfert-Rochereau and
then changing to RER line B to Châtelet-Les Halles in
the city center, traveling time approx. 40 mins. With
Air France coaches departing every 15 mins via Gare
Montparnasse to the Invalides station, traveling time
approx. 60 mins (www.carsairfrance.com). A cab ride
to downtown Paris costs approx. € 35 and takes

about 30 mins (extra charge of approx. 15 % from
7 pm to 7 am and on weekends).

By Train

There are six terminal stations in Paris: Gare St-La-
zare, Gare du Nord, Gare de l'Est, Gare de Lyon, Gare
d'Austerlitz and Gare Montparnasse, depending from
which direction you are traveling from. All terminal
stations have direct access to the Metro or the RER.

Further Railway Information
SNCF: Phone: +33 / 8 / 36 35 35 35, www.sncf.fr
Thalys: www.thalys.com

Immigration and Customs Regulations

European citizens need a valid identity card for traveling to France. For EU citizens there are virtually no
custom regulations. Every person at the age of 17
or older is allowed to carry goods for personal needs
duty-free, e.g. 800 cigarettes, 400 cigarillos, 200
cigars, 1 kg of tobacco, 10 l of liquor, 90 l of wine
and 110 l of beer.

INFORMATION

Tourist Information

Office du Tourisme de Paris
25, rue des Pyramides
75001 Paris
Phone: +33 / 8 / 92 68 30 00
www.parisinfo.com
June–Oct opened daily from 9 am to 7 pm, Nov–May,
Mon–Sat 10 am to 7 pm, Sun 11 am to 7 pm
Amongst others there are offices at the Gare du Nord
station, at Carrousel du Louvre and at Place du Tertre
in Montmartre.

City Magazines

Every Wednesday the event calendars **Pariscope** and **L'Officiel des Spectacles** with information on movies, theaters and concerts as well as exhibition schedules and opening hours are published. The monthly magazine **Time Out** as well as the gastronomy guide **Time Out Eating & Drinking** are published in English.

Websites

General
www.parisinfo.com – Website of the Paris Tourist Information (EN)
www.paris.fr – Official website of the city (FR, EN)

Going Out
www.eatinparis.com – Online restaurant guide (FR, EN)
www.parissi.com – Concerts, exhibitions, restaurants, bars and clubs (FR)
www.parisvoice.com – Scene guide with tips from the editorial staff and calendar of events (EN)
www.timeout.com/paris – Restaurants and bars, shopping, nightlife, calendar of events (EN)

Art and Culture
www.legeniedelabastille.net – Artists and galleries in the Bastille district (FR)
www.monum.fr – Presentation of national architectural monuments, e.g. Notre-Dame, Arc de Triomphe, Sainte-Chapelle, Panthéon (FR, EN)
www.parisbalades.com – Virtual walk through Paris with detailed information on the districts and architectural monuments (FR)
www.paris-pittoresque.com – The historical Paris with ancient pictures and engravings (FR)

www.picturalissime.com – Overview over Parisian museums with links (FR, EN)
www.theatreonline.com – Theater guide (FR)

Sports and Leisure
www.bercy.fr – Sports calendar and opening hours of the ice rink in the Palais Omnisports Paris-Bercy (FR)
www.boisdevincennes.com – Leisure activities in the large Bois de Vincennes park (FR)
www.disneylandparis.com – Website of the famous amusement park (EN)
www.pari-roller.com – Exploring Paris on inline skates, every Fri night for advanced skaters, every Sun afternoon for beginners (FR, EN)

Map
www.hot-maps.de – Interactive city map (D, EN)

Accommodation
www.all-paris-apartments.com – Accommodations in Paris (EN)
www.parishotels.com – Hotel search engine and online reservations (FR, EN)
www.paris-apts.com – Reservation of apartments (EN)
www.rentapart.com – Reservation of apartments (FR, EN)

Event Calendar
www.sortiraparis.com – Event calendar with booking service and annotated addresses (FR)

RECOMMENDED LITERATURE

Ernest Hemingway
A Moveable Feast. After World War I, Hemingway came to Paris as a newspaper correspondent. His memories take the reader to the Paris of the Twenties.

Victor Hugo
The Hunchback of Notre Dame. The tragic story of the hunchbacked, one-eyed Quasimodo and the beautiful Esmeralda takes places in medieval Paris around the Notre-Dame cathedral. In the third book, Hugo describes "A Bird's-eye View of Paris."

Gaston Leroux
The Phantom of the Opera. Terrible things happen in the Paris Opera. But who is responsible? The eerie love story was later used by Andrew Lloyd Webber for his famous musical.

Guy de Maupassant
Bel-Ami. Driven by extreme ambition and selfishness, the journalist Georges Duroy climbs his ladder to success—a brilliant portrayal of the corrupt press and finance business at the end of the 19th century.

Daniel Pennac
The Scapegoat / The Fairy Gunmother / Monsieur Malaussene / Write to Kill (and others). The Malaussene clan lives in the Parisian immigrant district Belleville. Benjamin, the oldest of the children, is constantly involved into peculiar crimes. As a born scapegoat he is always the main suspect.

Raymond Queneau
Zazie in the Metro. The precocious and rebellious country girl Zazie spends a weekend in Paris with her uncle Gabriel.

Georges Simenon
Maigret ... The famous pipe-smoking detective investigates in Paris in more than 60 crime novels. The investigations take him to the Paris of the ordinary people and into the nocturnal demimonde.

Andrea Weiss
Paris was a Woman. A richly illustrated portrait of the "Parisian women of the Rive Gauche," implying artists and authors like Colette, Gertrude Stein and Djuna Barnes.

Emile Zola
The Belly of Paris. After having fled from a prison camp, Florent lives with his brother Quenu and his wife Lisa—a detailed study of the Parisian district Les Halles.

CITY TOURS

Sightseeing Tours by Bus

Sightseeing buses
Several agencies offer guided city tours, thematic tours and trips, lasting from 1.5 hrs up to 1 day, from € 17.50/pers. There are opentopped double-decker buses circulating in the city center every 10–30 mins with the possibility to interrupt the tour at any tourist attraction, day ticket € 25/pers., two-day ticket € 28/pers.

Cityrama, 149, rue Saint-Honoré
Phone: +33 / 1 / 44 55 61 00, www.cityrama.com

Les Cars Rouges, 17, quai de Grenelle
Phone: +33 / 1 / 53 95 39 53, www.carsrouges.com

Paris l'OpenTour, 13, rue Auber
Phone: +33 / 1 / 42 66 56 56
www.paris-opentour.com

Paris Vision, 214, rue de Rivoli
Phone: +33 / 1 / 42 60 30 01, www.parisvision.com

Balabus
During the summer months on Sun, the municipal
bus line Balabus serves the main sites between Gare
du Lyon and Grande Arche de la Défense with the
option to interrupt the tour at any tourist attraction.
April–Sept, Sun 1.30 pm to 8.30 pm (last departure
from Gare du Lyon), departing every 15–30 mins,
duration approx. 70 mins, www.ratp.fr

Bicycle Tours
Guided half-and full-day bicycle tours as well as tours
in the evening are organized regularly by:

Paris à Vélo c'est sympa, 22, rue Alphonse-Baudin,
Phone: +33 / 1 / 48 87 60 01
www.parisvelosympa.com

Paris-Vélo, 2, rue du Fer à Moulin
Phone: +33 / 1 / 43 37 59 22
www.paris-velo-rent-a-bike.fr

Boat Tours

Seine Tours
Many of the attractions are situated along the bank
of the Seine River and the most comfortable way
to see them is by boat. Besides guided cruises of
about an hour (departing every 30–40 mins, approx.
€ 9/pers.), there are also special offers like dinner
and musical tours. The piers are situated near the
Eiffel Tower (Pont d'Iéna), at Pont de l'Alma and in
front of Notre-Dame, depending on the company.

Bateaux Parisiens, Phone: +33 / 8 / 25 01 01 01,
www.bateauxparisiens.com

Compagnie des Bateaux Mouches,
Phone: +33 / 1 / 42 25 96 10
www.bateauxmouches.com

Vedettes de Paris, Phone: +33 / 1 / 44 18 19 50,
www.vedettesdeparis.com

Batobus
www.batobus.com
Eight stops between Eiffel Tower and Jardin des Plan-
tes are approached by the river buses, departing every
30 mins. Day ticket € 11/pers., two-day ticket
€ 13/pers., five-day ticket € 16/pers.

Channel Tours
Boat tours on the Canal Saint-Martin are not that
well-known, but nevertheless very interesting. With
Canauxrama departing every day at 9.45 am and
14.30 pm from Port de l'Arsenal to Parc de la Villette
and vice versa, duration approx. 2.5 hrs, € 14/pers.
Combined Seine-Channel-Cruise with Paris Canal,
from the end of March until mid-Nov, departing every
day at 9.30 am from Musée d'Orsay and at 2.30 pm
from Parc de la Villette, duration approx. 3 hrs,
€ 16/pers.

Canauxrama, Phone: +33 / 1 / 42 39 15 00,
www.canauxrama.com

Paris Canal, Phone: +33 / 1 / 42 40 96 97,
www.pariscanal.com

Guided City Tours

Paris Balades

www.parisbalades.com
Tours through Paris with certified tourist guides. The website gives an overview of the program and the organizing companies.

Lookouts

A view over the roofs of Paris is always fascinating. The best opportunity therefore, without a doubt, still is the **Eiffel Tower** with its viewing platform at 276 m. Another very absorbing panorama can be seen from the roof terrace of the **Maine-Montparnasse Tower** at a height of 206 m. The view from the 110 m high **Grande Arche** is a little bit disappointing due to the distance between the monument and the city center. Other popular lower lookouts are **Notre-Dame, Arc de Triomphe, Pompidou Center, Panthéon, Institut du Monde Arabe** as well as the department stores **Galeries Lafayette** and **Printemps**, all offering an excellent view over Paris. The view from the **Sacré-Cœur** on the Montmartre Hill is popular, too. A breathtaking way to overview the city is a balloon ride in the safely fixed **Ballon de Paris** in the Parc André Citroën (www.aeroparis.com).

TICKETS & DISCOUNTS

Ticket Offices

FranceBillet

Phone: +33 / 8 / 92 69 21 92
http://otparis.francebillet.com
Online ticket service or via phone.

Fnac

Bastille, 4, place de la Bastille, Mon–Sat 10 am to 8 pm
Champs-Elysées, 74, avenue des Champs-Elysées, Mon–Sat 10 am to midnight, Sun 11 am to midnight
Forum des Halles, 1–7, rue Pierre-Lescot, Mon–Sat 10 am to 7.30 pm. Tickets for every kind of event.

Check Théâtre

33, Rue le Peletier, Phone: +33 / 1 / 42 46 72 40, www.check-theatre.com
Phone service Mon–Sat 10 am to 7 pm
Tickets for theater, opera, and concerts.

Kiosque Théâtre

Madeleine, 15, place de la Madeleine

Tour Montparnasse, Esplanade de la Tour Montparnasse. Tue–Sat 12.30 pm to 8 pm, Sun until 4 pm, sale of reduced-price tickets for theater, opera and concerts with performances on the same day.

Discounts

Paris Museum Passport

Free entry without waiting time to more than 60 museums and monuments in Paris and the surrounding areas. Available at the Office du Tourisme and the participating museums, as well as online at www.parisinfo.com. Two-day ticket € 30, four-day ticket € 45, six-day ticket € 60, www.parismuseumpass.fr.

Paris Visite

Free rides with RER, Metro, and buses as well as reduced entry fees for several sights. Available from one up to five days and for three, five or eight zones. The pass is on sale in every Metro station, as well as online at www.parisinfo.com. Day ticket for 1–3 zones € 8.50, www.ratp.fr.

GETTING AROUND IN PARIS

Local Public Transport

RATP – Transports en Île-de-France
Phone: +33 / 8 / 92 68 77 14
www.ratp.fr

The fastest and cheapest means of transport in Paris is the Metro, operating 16 lines from 5.30 am to 1 am. The Metro system is connected to five RER lines (A – E), which are serving the suburbs and the airports. Metro and RER (Réseau Express Régional) are completed by a dense bus network as well as streetcar lines in the outskirts. 42 night bus lines (noctilien) guarantee the transport for night revelers. The transport network is divided into zones. The purple ticket for 1–2 zones is valid for rides within the urban area and for the whole Metro network. The maximum duration of a ride in Metro with a single ticket is 2 hours with no changing restrictions, while the single ticket for the bus (ticket has to be canceled upon boarding !) is valid for one ride only without changing. Keep the tickets until the end of the ride, sometimes they are needed to open the exit gates. Single ticket 1–2 zones € 1.40, ticket for ten rides (carnet) € 10.90. Unlimited riding with 155 the day ticket Mobilis, 1–2 zones € 5.50 and Paris Visite (see above). Tickets on sale in every Metro station and in labeled shops, single tickets can be purchased from the bus driver. Route maps are available for download or interactive use on the website of the RATP.

Cabs

Alpha Taxi, Phone: +33 / 1 / 45 85 85 85
Taxis Bleus, Phone: +33 / 8 / 19 70 10 10
Taxis G7, Phone: +33 / 1 / 47 39 47 39

There are 3 different cab rates:
A (Mon–Sat 10 am to 5 pm within the urban area), B (Mon–Sat 5 pm to 10 am, Sun 7 am to midnight within the urban area, every day 7 am to 7 pm outskirts and airports), C (all other times and in the surrounding areas). Minimum rate € 5.20, extra charge for more than two pieces of baggage and for rides from or to rail stations or airports.

Velib' (Bicycle self-service)
20'600 bicycles over 1450 stations (1 every 300 meters) all around the city. Free the first 30 min, then € 1 to 4 for additional half hours.
Phone: +33 / 1 / 30 79 79 30
www.velib.paris.fr

FESTIVALS & EVENTS

This is just an excerpt from the program for the year.

Festival du Film des Femmes

At the end of March, International Women's Film Festival at the Maison des Arts de Créteil (www.filmsdefemmes.com).

Banlieues Bleues

At the beginning of March until the beginning of April, Jazz and world music festival in the northeastern suburbs (www.banlieuesbleues.org).

Foire du Trône

April/May, large funfair in the Bois de Vincennes (www.foiredutrone.com).

Fête de la Musique

21st June, Open air concerts of diverse genres (classical music, jazz and rock, world music, etc.) in the parks, squares and streets (www.fetedelamusique. culture.fr).

Course de Garçons de Café

At the end of June, race of the waiters and waitresses in working clothes and with a full tray. Starting and finishing point of the 8 km (5 miles) track is the Hôtel de Ville.

Fête Nationale

14th July, the evening before the national holiday there are public balls, processions and fireworks, on the 14th there is a huge military parade on the Champs-Elysées (www.14-juillet.cityvox.com).

Paris, Quartier d'Été

Mid July–end of Aug, comprehensive cultural program during the summer holidays with music, circus, dance, and theater.

Tour de France

At the end of July, finish of the famous cycle race on the Champs-Elysées (www.letour.fr).

Journées du Patrimoine

Mid Sept, open day in historical and public buildings (www.jp.culture.fr).

Festival d'Automne

Mid Sept–mid Dec, music, theater, and movie festival on several Parisian stages (www.festival-automne.com).

Nuit Blanche

At the beginning of Oct, a night full of cultural events.

USEFUL NOTES

Money

National currency: Euro (€)

Bank and credit cards: Money can be withdrawn at cash machines with Maestro-Card and other common credit cards and many hotels, restaurants, and shops accept credit cards.

Emergency

Police: Phone: 17

Ambulance (SAMU): Phone: 15

Fire Department: Phone: 18

Opening hours

Banks: Mon–Fri 9 am to 5 pm, some banks close during midday from 12.30 pm to 2 pm.

Shops: Normally Mon–Sat from 9 am to 7 pm, supermarkets usually longer. Smaller shops close during midday and on Mon. Bakers and butchers open on Sun mornings.

Museums: Usually from 9/10 am to 5/6 pm, one day in the week until 9/10 pm. Closing day is mostly Mon or Tue, smaller museums close during midday.

Restaurants: Lunch from noon until 1.30 pm, dinner approx. 8 pm to 10.30 pm.

Costs & Money

Paris is one of the most expensive metropolises of the world. One night in a simple hotel for two persons in a double-bed room (without breakfast) costs approx. € 100. A three course menu for lunch costs approx. € 20 and for dinner € 30. The prices for a coffee, a soft drink or a beer are between € 4 and 5.

Smoking

It is prohibited to smoke in public buildings, Metro stations, public means of transport and in restaurants and cafés.

When to go

Paris is worth a trip (visit) at every time of the year. During winter, temperatures hardly fall below the freezing point, although there is plenty of rain during Jan and Feb. During the French summer vacations in July and Aug the city is not that hectic, because many locals leave the town. But during midsummer some restaurants go on vacation too. The best months for visiting Paris are May, June and Sept.

Security

Paris does not differ much from other European cities; the normal precautions have to be taken. At night, remote and poorly-lit areas have to be avoided. Tourists should be aware of pickpockets in the Metro, in stations and at flea markets.

Phone Calls

Dialing code Paris: In France the dialing code forms part of the ten-digit phone number and is always marked, even in local calls.

Calling from abroad: +33 + desired phone number without 0

Calling from Paris: country code + area code without 0 + desired phone number

Directory assistance: Phone: 118 218

Public telephone boxes work with telephone or credit cards. The telephone cards can be purchased in kiosks or tobacco stores.

Tipping

Service and taxes are included in all prices. In hotels, restaurants, or cabs, satisfied clients can tip 5–10 % of the charged amount.

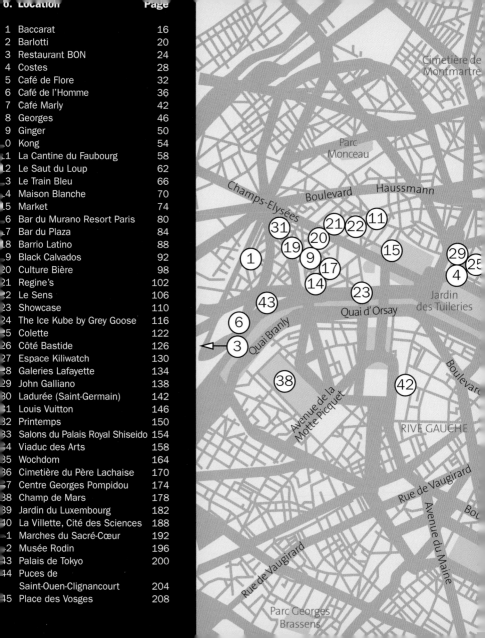

6. Location — Page

teNeues' new Cool Guide series

ISBN 978-3-8327-9293-0

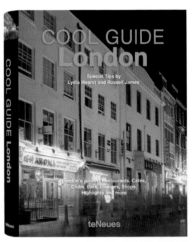

ISBN 978-3-8327-9294-7

ISBN 978-3-8327-9295-4

ISBN 978-3-8327-9296-1

Size: **15 x 19 cm**, 6 x 7 ½ in., 224 pp., **Flexicover**, c. 250 color photographs,
Text: English / German / French / Spanish
www.teneues.com

Other titles by teNeues

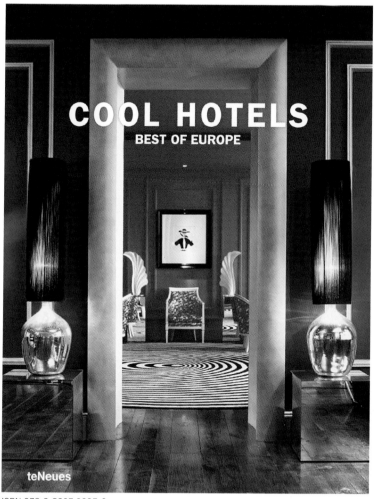

ISBN 978-3-8327-9235-0

Size: **25.6 x 32.6 cm**, 10 x 12⅞ in., 396 pp., **Hardcover with jacket**, c. 650 color photographs,
Text: English / German / French / Spanish / Italian
www.teneues.com

Other titles by teNeues

ISBN 978-3-8327-9309-8

ISBN 978-3-8327-9274-9

ISBN 978-3-8327-9237-4

ISBN 978-3-8327-9247-3

ISBN 978-3-8327-9234-3

ISBN 978-3-8327-9308-1

ISBN 978-3-8327-9243-5

ISBN 978-3-8327-9230-5

ISBN 978-3-8327-9248-0

Size: **15 x 19 cm**, 6 x 7 ½ in., 224 pp., **Flexicover**, c. 200 color photographs,
Text: English / German / French / Spanish / Italian
www.teneues.com